CW00849775

beyond SANITY
and MADNESS

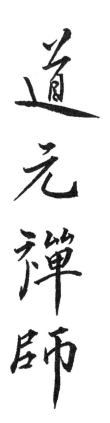
道元禅師

beyond SANITY and MADNESS

The Way of
Zen Master Dogen

by
Dennis Genpo Merzel

Introduction and calligraphy
by Hakuyu Taizan Maezumi, Roshi

Charles E. Tuttle Co., Inc.
Boston · Rutland, Vermont · Tokyo

Published by Charles E. Tuttle Company, Inc. of Rutland, Vermont, and Tokyo, Japan with editorial offices at 153 Milk Street, Boston, Massachusetts 02109

© 1994 Kanzeon, Inc.

All rights reserved. No part of this publication including artwork may be reproduced, stored in a retrieval system or transmitted in any form or by any means, electronic, mechanical, photocopying, recording, or otherwise, without prior written permission from Charles E. Tuttle Company, Inc.

The publishers have given permission to use material from the following works: From "Only Buddha and Buddha: Yuibutsu Yobutsu" translated by Ed Brown and Kazuaki Tanahashi from Moon in a Dewdrop: Writings of Zen Master Dogen edited by Kazuaki Tanahashi, copyright © 1985 by the San Francisco Zen Center. Reprinted by permission of North Point Press, a division of Farrar, Straus & Giroux, Inc. From "Yuibutsu Yobutsu," "Bodaisatta Shishobo," and "Bendowa" in Shobogenzo, translated by Kosen Nishiyama, © 1983, by Nakayama Shobo. From Two Zen Classics: Mumonkan and Hekiganroku trans. and edit. by Katsuki Sekida © 1977, and Zen Master Dogen by Yuho Yokoi with Daizen Victoria © 1976, both reprinted by permission of John Weatherhill, Inc. From Zen Comments on the Mumonkan by Zenkei Shibayama, © 1974, by Harper and Row. From Cutting Through Spiritual Materialism by Chögyam Trungpa, © 1973 by Chögyam Trungpa. Reprinted by arrangement with Shambhala Publications, P.O. Box 308, Boston MA 02117. From Eastern Buddhist, vol vi/2, 1973 a translation of Dogen Zenji's Fukanzazengi trans. by Waddell and Masao, © 1973, by the Eastern Buddhist Society, Otani University. From The Record of Rinzai trans. by Irmgard Schloegl, © 1975, and The Zen Teaching of Huang Po trans. and edit. by John Blofeld, © 1971, by the The Buddhist Society, London. From Dogen Zen trans. by Shohaku Okamura, © 1988, by the Kyoto Soto Zen Center.

Library of Congress Cataloging-in-Publication Data
Merzel, Dennis Genpo, 1944–
   Beyond sanity and madness: the way of Zen master Dogen / Dennis Genpo Merzel; introduction and calligraphy by Hakuyu Taizan Maezumi.
   p. cm.   — (Tuttle library of enlightenment)
   ISBN 0–8048–3035–5 (pbk.)
   1. Dōgen, 1200–1253. I. Title. II. Series.
BQ9449.D657M47 1994
294.3'927'092—dc20   94–34898
                                                            CIP

First Edition
1 3 5 7 9 10 8 6 4 2

Printed in the United States of America (EB)

Frontispiece: "Dogen Zenji" by Hakuyu Taizan Maezumi Roshi

To my teacher, Maezumi Roshi,
&
To all members of Kanzeon Sangha
for their continuous support and devotion
through a very challenging period
of our practice together
&
To those who helped
create the challenges

Mumon's Zen Warnings

—·—·—·—·—◈—·—·—·—·—

To observe the regulations and keep to the rules is tying oneself without a rope. To act freely and unrestrainedly just as one wishes is to do what heretics and demons would do. To recognize mind and purify it is the false Zen of silent sitting. To give rein to oneself and ignore interrelating conditions is to fall into the abyss. To be alert and never ambiguous is to wear chains and an iron yoke. To think of good and evil belongs to heaven and hell. To have a Buddha view and a Dharma view is to be confined in two iron mountains. He who realizes it as soon as a thought arises is one who exhausts his energy. To sit blankly in quietism is the practice of the dead. If one proceeds, he will go astray from the principle. If one retreats, he will be against the Truth. If one neither progresses nor retreats, he is a dead man breathing. Now tell me, what will you do? Work hard and be sure to attain "it" in this life, lest you have eternal regret.

Table of Contents

Preface

I wish to express my heartfelt appreciation to all Dharma teachers who have devoted their lives to transmitting the precious gift of the Buddha-dharma to the present generation in the West. My deepest desire is to support this delicate and difficult process, and with that in mind I have been working with students throughout Europe and America for more than fifteen years.

My intention in this book is to explore three major factors that are vital to the survival of the Zen spirit: the awakening of the One Buddha-mind, its mind-to-mind transmission, and its manifestation in our culture. Zen is still fragile in the West, and I am very concerned that attempts to make it more accessible by adjusting it to society's norms could easily dilute the essence of the teaching. It is even possible that through these well-intentioned efforts the practice could wither before it has a real chance to take root in our culture.

Zen Master Dogen was facing a similar situation in Japan seven hundred years ago. It was out of his deep commitment to the transmission of the true Dharma that he wrote the fascicles discussed in this book. Only by practicing zazen under a teacher, with the same wholehearted dedication and faith that Dogen Zenji brought to his own practice, can each one of us realize for ourselves what he realized.

This book does not offer any sort of scholarly analysis of Dogen Zenji's teaching, but rather discusses the essential features in his vision of Zen training and practice. The issues addressed in the three fascicles range from basic points concerning Zen training (*Gakudo Yojinshu*), through transcendental Wisdom and its transmission from teacher to student ("Yuibutsu Yobutsu"), to the compassion that arises out of awakened Mind for the benefit of all beings ("Bodaisatta Shishobo"). For Dogen Zenji, training in zazen, the attainment of realization, and compassionate action are different aspects of one indivisible reality.

Dogen Zenji's teaching is known as *Saijojo Zen*, the Supreme and Ultimate Way, which embraces and yet transcends the Three Vehicles—Hinayana, Mahayana, and Buddhayana. The Way of Zen Master Dogen is to forget oneself and to go beyond all dualistic concepts of sanity and madness, good and evil, enlightened and deluded, Buddha and ordinary person.

I wish to express my deepest gratitude first of all to my teacher, Maezumi Roshi, for his wisdom, patience and perseverance in transmitting the Buddha-dharma to the Western world, for his scholarly Introduction, and for the beautiful calligraphies that ornament this book; and to the two editors, Anton Tenkei Coppens and Stephen Muho Proskauer, who worked long and hard assisting me in writing this book. It could not have been written without them. I also wish to thank Monique Koren

Vervecken and Kenneth Hebson for many hours of typing, Karen Tate for editorial help, and Paul Weiss for his encouragement and his financial contribution to this book. Furthermore, I wish to express my deep appreciation to the many people—my teachers, Dharma brothers and sisters, colleagues and friends—and especially to my family, who have supported me over the years and made many sacrifices: Ben Merzel, Lillian Merzel, Carol Merzel Jacobs, Lynn Shozen McNamara, Brenda Hobai Liu, Tai Merzel, Nicole Merzel, and Catherine Genno Pages.

Dennis Genpo Merzel

Foreword

This book consists of three interrelated parts. The first part gives commentary on *Gakudo Yojinshu*, the second deals with "Yuibutsu Yobutsu," and the third discusses "Bodaisatta Shishobo." Maezumi Roshi's Introduction provides background information about these three essays by Zen Master Dogen.

Throughout the book, Dogen Zenji's words are printed in italics and commentary appears in roman type. In the main body of the book, Dogen Zenji's text is not given as a whole, but divided up into short sections for purposes of discussion. The complete translations of the three fascicles are printed in their entirety in the appendices. Many of the Zen Buddhist terms employed in the text are briefly defined where they first appear, and there is a glossary of Zen terminology following the appendices to further assist the reader. Information about books and authors cited once only is given in the notes which appear at the end of each chapter. Bibliographical information about more frequently cited published works can be found in the list of references at the back of the book.

At some Zen centers, the word "Patriarch" is no longer used because it is associated with the idea of patriarchy. However, we have been unable to find a term of neutral gender to convey the meaning of both "esteemed leader" and "ancestor," so the historical title "Patriarch" has been retained in this book.

We wish to acknowledge the cooperation of Weatherhill in granting permission to quote the Yokoi translation of *Gakudo Yojinshu* from *Zen Master Dogen* and of Farrar, Straus & Giroux, Inc., for permission to quote the Tanahashi and Brown translation of "Yuibutsu Yobutsu" from *Moon in a Dewdrop: Writings of Zen Master Dogen*. Efforts have been made to secure permission from Nakayama Shobo for quoting the Nishiyama translation of "Bodaisatta Shishobo" from *Shobogenzo: The Eye and Treasury of the True Law*. While these three translations have been used as the primary basis for the commentaries, the author has paraphrased certain words and phrases in each of them. Japanese forms of most proper names have been used, and the texts have been printed in accord with the style of this book. Therefore the translations do not appear precisely as originally published.

We wish to thank all the members of the entire Kanzeon Sangha who gave their wholehearted support to this project. Most of all, we would like to express deep appreciation to Genpo Sensei for spreading the Dharma throughout Europe and the United States. We are profoundly grateful for the opportunity to train and live with him, sharing the gift of the Dharma, the living expression of the teachings set forth in this book.

Anton Tenkei Coppens
Stephen Muho Proskauer

Introduction

by Hakuyu Taizan Maezumi, Roshi

—·—·—·—·—·—◆—·—·—·—·—·—

Gakudo Yojinshu

In 1225, Master Dogen (1200-1253) received Dharma transmission from Zen Master T'ien-t'ung Ju-ching (Japanese Tendo Nyojo). Master Dogen returned to Japan from China in 1227, and six years later he established Kosho-ji, the first formal Zen monastery in the Soto tradition and the first to hold a 90-day summer *ango* (practice period). It was during this *ango* that Master Dogen began to write, in Japanese, the now-famous series of writings known as *Shobogenzo*. The first two fascicles of Shobogenzo were written during this time: the "Makahanyaharamitsu" at the start of *ango*; "Genjokoan" about a month later. Master Dogen wrote *Gakudo Yojinshu*, in which he elucidated ten points or guidelines for practicing the Buddha Way, about a year later. The epilogue to the third point is dated March 9, 1234; the sixth point, April 5, 1234. Although the other points are not dated, we can guess that they were written around the same time. While Master Dogen's teachings are close-ly identified with monastic training, these fascicles were studied by both monks and lay persons.

First published in 1357 by Abbot Donki of Eihei-ji, the *Gakudo Yojinshu* is the oldest publication in the history of the Soto School and holds a special significance as the backbone document of Soto practice. It is in *Gakudo Yojinshu* that Master Dogen sets forth how the "correctly transmitted Buddha-dharma" (which he first proclaimed in "Bendowa" in 1231) was to be practiced by the monks living together in his newly established monastery.

At that time, Buddhism was commonly understood by society-at-large in terms of satisfying such needs as curing ill-nesses, improving one's life, and becoming reborn in the Western Paradise. It was within this common context of practice that Master Dogen propounded a genuine Buddhism that emphasized continuous practice and that practice and realization were not two, but one. He emphasized the practice of the Buddha Way, which he called "just practicing the Buddha-dhar-ma for the sake of Buddha-dharma."

It is questionable just how much Master Dogen's emphasis on and firm conviction of the right Dharma, derived from the aspect of nondualism as expressed in this fascicle, was actually perceived and appreciated while he lived. Ten years after the founding of Kosho-ji, Master Dogen moved to Eihei-ji. It is believed that this move was prompted in part by attempts to suppress Dogen's teachings and may also have been an indica-tion of just how difficult it was to practice his "right Dharma."

There is a tendency for *Gakudo Yojinshu* to be used as instruction for beginners because the points of practice are short and concise. However, when each point is carefully examined, we begin to realize the difficulty of practicing according to

Introduction

Master Dogen's teaching and that this text is for the study of senior practitioners rather than for less-experienced persons.

Yuibutsu Yobutsu

The original manuscript of "Yuibutsu Yobutsu" has been lost, but the essay first appeared in the 95-fascicle edition of *Shobogenzo*, edited by Zen Master Kozen, the 35th Abbot of Eihei-ji (in the era of Genroku, 1688-1704). Until that time, "Yuibutsu Yobutsu" was part of the *Esoteric Shobogenzo*, a collection of 28 fascicles stored at Eihei-ji. It also appeared as fascicle no. 38 in another version of *Shobogenzo* and was replaced by "Katto" or "Spiritual Entanglement" in a later version. The reasons for this replacement are unknown, but include the possibility that "Yuibutsu Yobutsu" was not originally written by Dogen Zenji. There is no date as to when this fascicle was written. The only date associated with it is 1288, when it was transcribed or copied.

The title "Yuibutsu Yobutsu" is from the quotation that Master Dogen uses in the fascicle's first paragraph: "only a Buddha and a Buddha thoroughly master it." This line appears in "Skillful Means," the second chapter of the *Lotus Sutra*, which was valued by Master Dogen as the most important discourse in Buddhism and to which he referred most often among his various writings. Although the work of translation raises many complex issues, I should like to touch briefly upon the translation of this quotation. It is very important to understand Master Dogen's intention in using this line.

In this book, Genpo Sensei uses the Tanahashi and Brown translation published by the San Francisco Zen Center. We also have another version by Nishiyama, which Genpo Sensei quotes in his commentary. The versions, which complement each other, are as follows:

Nishiyama: "Only a Buddha can transmit to a Buddha, and only a Buddha understands the truth entirely." (in Dogen Zenji, *Shobogenzo*, translated by Kosen Nishiyama, Vol. 3, Tokyo: Nakayama Shobo, 1983, p.129)

Tanahashi and Brown: "Because it is realized by Buddhas alone, it is said, 'Only a Buddha and a Buddha can thoroughly master it.'" (in *Moon in a Dewdrop: Writings of Zen Master Dogen*, edited by Kazuaki Tanahashi, San Francisco: North Point Press, 1985, p.161)

The original passage as presented in the Leon Hurvitz translation of *The Lotus Sutra* (*Scripture of the Lotus Blossom of the Fine Dharma*, translated from the Chinese of Kumarajiva, New York: Columbia University Press, 1976, p. 22), consists of two important clauses: ". . . as for the immeasurable, unlimited dharmas that have never been before, the Buddha has perfected them all. Cease, Sariputra, we need speak no more. Why is this? [clause 1:] Concerning the prime, rare, hard-to-understand dharmas, which the Buddha has perfected, [clause 2:] only a Buddha and a Buddha can exhaust their reality . . ."

Master Dogen uses "Only a Buddha and a Buddha" ("Yuibutsu Yobutsu") as the fascicle's title and uses "only a Buddha and a Buddha thoroughly master it" in the body of the fascicle. He refers to "the ultimate reality of all beings" as "it." This "it" is no other than "the prime, rare, hard-to-understand dharmas that the Buddha realized," the central theme of the *Lotus Sutra*. Master Dogen further expresses "it," "the ultimate reality of all beings," as "all beings *are* the ultimate reality." By not quoting these phrases together, Master Dogen prompts us to avoid merely conceptualizing this famous passage.

Introduction

Master Dogen's first sentence, "The Buddha-dharma cannot be understood by a 'person,'" is almost unapproachable through our normal level of conscious awareness. It rejects our usual dualistic and discriminative perspectives. The implication of "person" is that all dharmas, all beings, *are* the ultimate reality; they *are* the appearance of Buddha. Every thing *is* the perfected form of realization and cannot be understood as the object of discriminative conscious functions. A human being, or "person," is one who thinks, speculates, analyzes, and compares oneself and others in dichotomous ways. In the same fashion, such a one tries to realize Buddha by attempting to become Buddha, an object to be achieved. Through these typical but artificial human efforts, we can neither realize Buddhahood nor confirm ourselves as Buddha, *as Bodhi*, as the Way itself.

In referring to the passage, "only a Buddha and a Buddha thoroughly master it," Master Dogen intended to reveal ultimate reality as the focal point for practitioners on how to live one's life as the manifestation of "a Buddha and a Buddha." "Only a Buddha transmits to a Buddha thoroughly" should be appreciated and penetrated as Master Dogen's admonition to each of us, as practitioners of the Buddha Way, to live in accord with the ultimate reality of standing, sitting, walking, and lying down in our everyday life.

We Zen practitioners are well acquainted with such expressions as "The Mind is the Buddha," "This body becomes a Buddha," "Directly pointing out one's mind, seeing the nature, one becomes Buddha," or "Straightforwardly enter the realm of Buddha," etc. In order to reveal such a realm of existence, we must first know the unreckonable abyss that lies between "person" and "Buddha." This disparity cannot be dissolved by artificial and dualistic means. How can we dissolve this seemingly infinite boundary between "person" and "Buddha," between delusion and enlightenment?

Such an attempt is impossible to accomplish as a "person," and it has indeed been a challenge for Genpo Sensei to present commentaries on this fascicle. Having so few reference materials available in English makes this task even more difficult. This is our challenge: how to drop off this incomprehensible confinement and reveal "one's own original face that has never been hidden" which Master Dogen explores in this fascicle.

Bodaisatta Shishobo

Written in 1244, "Bodaisatta Shishobo" ("The Four Benevolent Ways of the Bodhisattva") elucidates practices of *dana* (giving). These practices are observed from four perspectives: first, almsgiving in a comprehensive or inclusive way; second, loving words in terms of speech; third, beneficial actions in terms of conduct and faith; and fourth, identification with others as the expression of compassion. Almsgiving is also placed first in the six and ten *paramitas* of the Mahayana tradition. These benevolent ways are practices of *sanmitsu*, or practices of the body, mouth, and mind.

Prior to Shakyamuni himself, *dana* was practiced in the Hindu tradition. During the time of Shakyamuni Buddha, these four benevolent ways were expounded and recommended for both monks and laity. It is also written that these benevolent actions were practiced by Shakyamuni Buddha during his past lives as a Bodhisattva and also appear as teachings in the *Agama Sutra*. When Buddhism entered the age of Mahayana, these benevolent actions were expounded as Mahayana practices and incorporated in the Mahayana sutras such as the *Prajnaparamita*

Sutra, the *Vimalakirti Sutra*, the *Avatamsaka Sutra*, and the *Lotus Sutra*. In fact, these actions are common practices not unique to Mahayana Buddhism, but widely applied in any time, place, and culture.

There are different kinds of *dana*. In the Mahayana tradition, it is generally said that there is the *dana* of material things, of the Dharma, and of no-fear. There are eight kinds of giving of material things expounded in the *Agama Sutra*. One gives: (1) with expectation of some kind of immediate return; (2) to avoid undesirable results or happenings; (3) as repayment for past debts; (4) for some desired future benefit; (5) as a family custom; (6) in order to be reborn in the heavens; (7) so that others will think favorably of oneself; and (8) for the sake of realizing enlightenment. The first seven kinds of *dana* involve giving material things for gain and comfort; only in the eighth point alone is giving directed towards liberation.

Dana also involves the giving of nonmaterial things such as the Dharma. Among these is the giving of "emptiness and tranquillity of the Three Wheels": the giver, receiver, and thing given are empty. This kind of benevolent action, the *dana* of genuine compassion or no-fear that transcends even enlightenment, is "true *dana*."

Almsgiving, the first of the four benevolent ways, is widely practiced not only in Buddhism, but also in other religious traditions. But particularly in the Mahayana tradition, acts of compassion done with the intention of "benefiting others" is a primary characteristic. In the *Shobogenzo* fascicle "Bodhi-citta" (Bodhi-mind), Master Dogen teaches that benefiting others means "to raise one's Bodhi-mind by helping others to the other shore before crossing over oneself." In the sutra *Kanromon*, which is chanted daily in Soto monasteries, there is a line that is repeated over and over: "*Om bodhi-citta utpadayami.*" It means "to renew and refresh the Bodhi-mind in order to practice soundly." This *Bodhi-citta* is the core of Buddhist faith and is the source of inspiration for practice.

Master Dogen repeatedly stresses the importance of *Bodhi-citta* (in Japanese, *doshin*, or "the mind of the Way") throughout his many writings. Regarding this mind, Master Dogen writes that one should, primarily, contemplate the impermanence of all beings. Then, realizing the impersonal, the "no-I," live in accord with this understanding, holding the Dharma in the highest esteem. In *Gakudo Yojinshu*, Master Dogen says that "the Way is to practice the Buddha-dharma for the sake of the Buddha-dharma." In other words, without "I," we *live* the ungraspable Dharma. Secondly, he emphasizes taking refuge in the Three Treasures—the Buddha, Dharma, and Sangha—and maintaining undefiled faith. With these practices as our foundation, we raise *Bodhi-citta*. We raise the heart of saving beings by helping others over before we ourselves cross to the other shore, thereby engaging in the highest form of almsgiving.

The Four Great Vows are the general vows of the Bodhisattva. In the first vow, we vow to liberate all beings, regardless of their number. Master Dogen proclaims that from the very first, *this Bodhi-mind*, the raising of this vow with our whole body and mind, is itself the beginner's mind. And this raising or practice of the beginner's mind is itself *honsho*, "intrinsic realization." He proclaims that "*honsho* is manifested even in beginner's mind." Furthermore, this Bodhi-mind is the Way of "practice and realization are not separate, but one."

Prior to Dogen Zenji, almsgiving as based on the ancient doctrine of the four benevolent ways had not been interpreted to this extent. Master Dogen reminds us to appreciate these old teachings from the Bodhisattva's perspectives and to continually refresh our own integrity as embodied in these great vows of benefiting oneself and others.

Genpo Sensei, the teacher of the Kanzeon Sangha, presents his commentary on these four benevolent actions. As taught in the *Lotus Sutra*, Kanzeon Bodhisattva's original vow is to benefit all beings by transforming his/her body into thirty-three or numberless forms. Genpo Sensei, a follower of Kanzeon, offers his comments for your consideration. It will be most rewarding for him if these comments stimulate your own practice and cause you to confirm your vows. I offer you my sincere encouragement in the genuine practice of the Buddha Way.

H. T. Maezumi
Los Angeles

Gakudo Yojinshu

Points to Watch in Practicing the Way

Points to Watch in Practicing the Way
Point One

The Need to Awaken to the Bodhi-mind

The Bodhi-mind is known by many names; all refer to the One Mind of the Buddha. The Venerable Nagarjuna said, "The mind that sees into the flux of arising and decaying and recognizes the transient nature of the world is also known as the Bodhi-mind." [1]

Like the vast blue sky, the One Mind of the Buddha defies all comprehension and can never be fathomed. It can only be realized by a Buddha. The One Mind is unborn and undying; yet it observes the flux of arising and decaying and recognizes the transient nature of all phenomena. Earth, grass, trees, walls, tiles, and pebbles all engage in Buddha's activity. Awakening to the One Mind means to embrace impermanence and transcend all dualistic notions of life and death, self and others, good and evil. It is the only way to go beyond the sanity and madness of the world.

People suffer from both sanity and madness because they have not yet realized their essential nature, which is nothing but the One Mind of the Buddha. Awakening to the Buddha-mind is complete liberation, putting an end to all suffering and confusion.

Bodhi-mind raises the aspiration to awaken all sentient beings. Dogen Zenji said: "Every Buddha and each Tathagata has the wonderful ability to attain supreme and perfect enlightenment; they transmit that enlightenment from one to another without alteration. This ability transcends and is not bound by any human devices—it is *jijuyu samadhi*, the proper method and standard of the transmission from Buddha to Buddha. To achieve this *samadhi*, you must enter the true gate of zazen—the best method of manifesting enlightenment."[2]

Why, then, is temporary dependence on this mind called the Bodhi-mind? When the transient nature of the world is recognized, the ordinary selfish mind does not arise; neither does the mind that seeks for fame and profit.

When the Bodhi-mind is awakened and the transient nature of the world is recognized, the whole notion of possession no longer has meaning. Because all things are empty, there is nothing to cling to. Trying to accumulate wealth, fame, position, or security seems ridiculous and futile. It only makes sense to the ordinary mind. Only those with deluded understanding act as if it were possible to secure their existence and make it into something permanent and substantial. By trying to establish sanity, they live a life of madness.

Aware that time waits for no man, train as though you were attempting to save your head from being enveloped in flames.

4

Reflecting on the transient nature of body and life, exert yourself just as the Buddha Shakyamuni did when he raised his foot.

The nature of the world is transient and time waits for no one. The opportunity to accomplish the Way can easily be lost. To accomplish the Way means to awaken to the complete interdependence of all things, to the whole universe as One Mind. This realization makes it impossible to continue to think dualistically, to want only what is good for oneself without considering what is good for the whole. What naturally arises is the Bodhi-mind, the mind that seeks to awaken all sentient beings. Ordinary selfish views simply do not arise. Consider how the right hand cooperates with the left hand without jealousy or envy. Likewise the liver would never become upset because the heart gets more attention.

Dogen Zenji is exhorting us to practice as if our head were enveloped in flames. This means to practice zazen single-mindedly, dropping off body and mind, realizing the Way of all the Buddhas. When you sit and reflect on impermanence, you realize that this life is a gift from countless beings who have offered their lives so that you can live. When you really look into the transient nature of life, a deep sense of gratitude and appreciation naturally arises, and you realize that you will never be able to repay your debt to all existence. Your own life and this body which has consumed so much in so few years will not go very far in repayment of this debt. A feeling of unworthiness and humility may come up when you discover this. But the sense of unworthiness is not at all negative; in fact, it is a great affirmation, because it inspires you to make the inexhaustible vow to serve all sentient beings, lifetime after lifetime.

Although you hear the flattering call of the god Kimnara and the kalavinka bird, pay no heed, regarding them as merely the evening breeze blowing in your ears. Even though you see a face as beautiful as that of Mosho or Seishi, think of them as merely the morning dew blocking your vision.[3]

Once you commit yourself to the Way, it is important not to be seduced by the countless objects of your desire. Regard them all as merely an evening breeze blowing past your face or as the morning dew on the grass. These are all temporary and unsubstantial by their very nature—here one moment, gone the next. Only single-minded and wholehearted devotion to zazen can preserve the Buddha-dharma.

Dogen Zenji's teacher, Tendo Nyojo, had this to say: "Death and disease may strike tonight or on the morrow. With time so short, how foolish it is to fail to practice the Buddha-dharma and to waste your time in sleep! This is what brings the decline of the Buddha-dharma. When it flourishes in all corners of the world, monks in all monasteries concentrate solely on sitting meditation. Because it is not encouraged these days, the Buddha-dharma is on the decline."[4]

When freed from the bondage of sound, color, and shape, you will naturally become one with the true Bodhi-mind. Since ancient times there have been those who have heard little of true Buddhism and others who have seen little of the sutras. Most of them have fallen into the pitfall of fame and profit, losing the essence of the Way forever. What a pity! How regrettable! This should be well understood.

Realizing the unsubstantiality of all things releases you from the bondage of sound, color, and form. By awakening

Bodhi-mind you realize that all things are empty and impermanent, and by seeing that all things are empty and impermanent you naturally become one with the Bodhi-mind. Impermanence and the transient nature of life are usually seen as negative, something to be feared and resisted; but it is precisely because everything is being born and dying continuously that you are already liberated. Even if you would like to be attached and stuck, you cannot. Even if you try to cling to the way things are and to what you possess, you cannot do so. Isn't this wonderful? Everything goes in its own time; you are free from all things, whether you wish to be or not. Most people fear loss of what they love and are attached to, but in actuality loss brings more freedom. Everyone is in a constant state of liberation, being born and dying countless times every second. There is no liberation apart from this cycle of birth and death. This very birth and death is nirvana.

Even though you have read the expedient or true teachings of excellent sutras or transmitted the esoteric and exoteric teachings, unless you forsake fame and profit you cannot be said to have awakened to the Bodhi-mind.

There are some who say that the Bodhi-mind is the highest supreme enlightenment of the Buddha, free from fame and profit.

Unless you forsake fame and profit you have not truly awakened the Bodhi-mind. It is simply that if you have awakened the Bodhi-mind, seeking fame and profit does not arise, neither do other selfish desires. Notions of good or bad are irrelevant. Being ignorant does not make one bad, only confused. Not seeking fame and profit does not make one good, only free.

A mother does not steal food from the mouth of her child. This doesn't necessarily make her a good mother; it is only natural for a mother not to do such a thing. Buddhas are like this, too; they see all sentient beings as not separate from themselves. They are not making any attempt to be good or righteous. They are only doing what comes naturally, which is awakening all sentient beings. It is only ordinary people who try to live up to dualistic criteria of good behavior, which does not make them necessarily bad, only foolish.

Others say that it is that which embraces the one billion worlds in a single moment of thought, or that it is the teaching that not a single delusion arises. Still others say that it is the mind that directly enters into the realm of the Buddha. These people, not yet understanding what the Bodhi-mind is, wantonly slander it. They are indeed far from the Way.

People who have not yet really awakened to the Bodhi-mind end up slandering the Way of complete relinquishment, not out of bad intentions, only out of ignorance. Being caught up in dualistic mind, they see things in a very deluded way. It is like a flock of geese honking; they make a lot of noise, but say nothing. These people are indeed far from the Way.

Dogen Zenji is not particularly denying the truth of any of the doctrines he refers to, but is criticizing people who have not undergone complete relinquishment and who repeat words of others without personal experience. Some Buddhist priests were so upset with his views that they tried to destroy him. He escaped just in time and moved deep into the mountains to establish his monastery, Eihei-ji.

Reflect on your ordinary mind, selfishly attached as it is to fame and profit. Is it endowed with the essence and appearance of the three thousand worlds in a single moment of thought? Has it experienced the teaching that not a single delusion arises? No, there is nothing there but the delusion of fame and profit, nothing worthy of being called the Bodhi-mind.

Everybody is looking for something—for money, fame, position, status, or a better relationship, for whatever they think is lacking. Even a monk sitting alone on a mountaintop may still be looking for something.

As far as Dogen Zenji is concerned, all forms of practice that are stained with ideas of gain are impure—not necessarily wrong, just impure. Pure practice can only happen when you let go of your fixation on fame and profit. Most of us, however, are goal-oriented, so we begin practicing in order to get better in one way or another. It may take years to awaken to the Truth that all striving is unnecessary because you lack nothing to begin with. Since the first time you sat down in zazen, enlightenment was already in complete realization. And yet without long and arduous training, this fact can never be realized.

When one believes that there is something to be attained, then enlightenment can easily be regarded as something solid and substantial. But the truth is, there is nothing to attain. Mind can never be grasped, because it doesn't exist outside the self; and when you look inward you can't find it there either. Bodhi-mind is no-mind, unborn and undying; it has no form or characteristics. Mind is just whatever it is, perfect and complete.

Of course everyone has flaws and imperfections; we all prove it over and over again. Nevertheless, our very life with all its flaws is perfect as it is. Nothing can be added to it or taken away, because it is the very life of the Buddha.

Although there have been Patriarchs since ancient times who have used secular means to realize enlightenment, none of them has been attached to fame and profit, or even Buddhism, let alone the ordinary world.

The Bodhi-mind is, as previously mentioned, that which recognizes the transient nature of the world—one of the four insights. It is utterly different from that referred to by madmen.

After you have let go of just about everything, then the Dharma itself can become an attachment. This can actually be dangerous. How many wars have been fought in the name of God, freedom or democracy? Buddhism, too, can be used as an excuse to do whatever we believe is right.

When you awaken to the Truth, you realize there is no Buddha, no Dharma, and no higher authority. It is the unchanging, undefiled *dharmakaya*—your life, which is changing constantly. Those who are seeking for some fixed idea or definition of it are completely off.

The deluded mind tries desperately to create a sense of security where none is possible. Standards of right and wrong are set up to avoid facing uncertainty. Bodhi-mind is the realization that there are no absolute norms. The desire to establish such standards in order to control one's life and that of others can only arise from lack of faith in the Way. Although there is a right and wrong for every given situation, it is only fanatics and madmen who try to determine for everyone else what they should or should not do.

The nonarising mind and the appearance of the one billion worlds are fine practices after having awakened to the Bodhi-mind. "Before" and "after," however, should not be confused. Simply forget the self and quietly practice the Way. This is truly the Bodhi-mind.

To wake up to Bodhi-mind turns everything right side up. What appeared as sanity before now seems to be sheer madness, and what was seen as madness before is now seen as sanity. In the silent sitting of zazen, body and mind are dropped off, and one realizes the identity of self and others. Zazen is the complete realization of self—self identified with others.

How incredible it would be if we would all just forget ourselves and quietly practice the Way! If we have the courage to just sit and do nothing, the Bodhi-mind is present. Those who observe the uncertainty of life eventually stop trying to control it.

If you are simply one with everything that appears, neither grasping nor rejecting anything, the separation between subject and object does not arise. It is only an illusion that drops away. The mind returns to its original nature, which is just like the vast blue sky.

When you sit in the traditional posture of zazen, you have the greatest capacity to respond appropriately to whatever arises. No matter what difficulties you encounter, the loss of a job or a relationship or the death of someone close, you will find that you can sit and face it all.

There is no enlightenment apart from practice, but enlightenment happens only when you truly realize that you are perfect and complete as you are. Once you have realized this beyond a shadow of a doubt, then you can truly practice just sitting without pursuing anything. Then whatever happens is the manifestation of the Buddha-dharma. This reveals complete faith in the Way; it is the heart of the teaching. If you practice the Buddha Way, everything will take care of itself.

The sixty-two viewpoints are based on self; so when egoistic views arise, just do zazen quietly, observing them. What is the basis of your body, its inner and outer possessions? You received your body, hair, and skin from your parents. The two droplets, red and white, of your parents, however, are empty from beginning to end; hence there is no self here. Mind, discriminating consciousness, knowledge, and dualistic thought bind life. What, ultimately, are exhaling and inhaling? They are not self. There is no self to be attached to. The deluded, however, are attached to self, while the enlightened are unattached. But still you seek to measure the self that is no self, and attach yourselves to arisings that are nonarising, neglecting to practice the Way. By failing to sever your ties with the world, you shun the true teaching and run after the false. Dare you say you are not acting mistakenly?

The sixty-two views mentioned here include all possible views that are based on the illusion of self. They can be divided into two major categories: one which states that the self is permanent and survives the death of the body; the other which sees death as complete extinction, the end of everything. All of these views are based on dualistic thinking and are therefore delusive.

The deluded mind clings to ideas in order to feel secure and right. To let go of these notions is almost impossible, especially the beliefs that seem most correct, as if it were more important to be right than liberated. Many people seem to prefer anxiety, depression, madness, or even death over the loss of their opinions. The awakened mind lets go of dualistic thinking and enjoys perfect freedom in all situations.

Dropping your opinions gives you the space to ask questions like: what is body and mind? When you look inside, what do you find? Is there really any fixed self? Questions like this are called *koans*. Of course they can arise naturally, but in Zen the teacher may choose a particular question for a student to work on. Koans have proven to be strong devices for cutting through the delusion of self and other, good and evil, enlightened and deluded.

Everyone originates from a sperm and an egg cell, which are unsubstantial from the beginning. Physics has taught us that the atoms that make up our body are more like patterns of energy than solid little entities. Shakyamuni Buddha came to basically the same realization twenty-five hundred years ago: life has no substance; all forms are empty. It is all movement. There is absolutely nothing fixed or permanent. The concept of the body as something solid and the mind as something lasting is only based on the belief that there is an entity called "self." If the body is not solid and the mind is not lasting, then who am I? Do I really exist or not?

The deluded, however, are attached to self and caught up in dualistic thinking, while the enlightened are unattached. This is the point: to give up attachment to self, to me and mine. The source of all suffering is attachment to self. The enlightened mind is no longer attached, because it makes no distinction between self and other. This comes from the realization that it is impossible to measure the self. There is no beginning and no end to it; it is unborn and undying. The deluded mind believes that discriminating is indispensable and desperately tries to substantiate the self, consolidating that which is formless by nature. Because this involves a lot of effort, we depend on each other to support this illusion. Society has conspired to cover up the fact that there is no self to begin with.

According to the Buddha we are being born and are dying faster than we can be aware of, something like eighty-four thousand times each second. To see life as one continuous existence is an illusion. Actually every particle in the body is disappearing and reappearing continuously. All existence is in constant flux.

While watching a movie you can get so involved that you forget that it is all an illusion. Quieting the mind and being attentive is like slowing down the projector, so that each frame can be seen separately. It enables one to realize how everything is constantly flickering in and out of existence. There are no objects; there is no fixed self.

Those who are afraid to sever their ties with the world out of fear of losing what is dear to them run after false teachings and follow people with dualistic understanding. Unable to bear the chaos of not knowing, they seek after quick cures for their distress and easy answers for their confusion, as if that could give meaning to a life that feels empty and meaningless. The fear of facing reality gives rise to dreams and fantasies which obscure the only Truth that can set them free: that there is no Truth—no enlightenment, no realization, and no Way. This is the great liberation.

When you truly realize this, beyond a shadow of a doubt, you have truly awakened Buddha-mind. This Buddha-mind is pure and clear from the beginning. In this mind there is no life or death, no doing or reaction to doing, no winning or losing. It is solitary and exquisite. If you enter this Dharma gate, you are the same as all the Buddhas. All good and evil, all doing and nondoing will be just like a dream.

Notes

[1] Nagarjuna, the 14th Zen Patriarch in India, lived around the 2nd or 3rd century. He is considered to have been the greatest Mahayana Buddhist philosopher of his era.

[2] Dogen Zenji, "Bendowa," in *Shobogenzo*, translated by Nishiyama, Volume One, 147.

[3] Kimnara: the heavenly god of music. Kalavinka: a Himalayan bird with a sweet call. Mosho and Seishi: two legendary women, symbols of beauty in ancient China.

[4] Kodera, 59.

Points to Watch in Practicing the Way
Point Two

The Need for Training
Upon Encountering the True Dharma

*A king's mind can often be changed as the result of advice
given by a loyal retainer. If the Buddhas and Patriarchs offer even
a single word, there will be none who remain unconverted. Only
wise kings, however, heed the advice of their retainers, and only
exceptional trainees listen to the Buddha's words.*

There are many people who encounter the Buddha-
dharma, but not all are receptive enough to hear the teaching
with an open mind. Since doubt about the meaning of life is a
driving force behind spiritual search, those who have gone
through great loss or despair are usually more eager. It is easy,
however, to lose this open-mindedness after some years of
practice and become satisfied with a shallow understanding.

One task of a good teacher is to keep students on the
edge and to challenge them to clarify their insight continuously. In the Zen tradition, koans are sometimes used for this
purpose. Although often misunderstood, koan study can be a

very strong medicine for those who are ready to receive it. It reveals an aspect of the teaching that may seem harsh, yet is highly effective in testing one's understanding. Much of this book is an attempt to convey the vigorous spirit of traditional koan training.

Let's take the case of Master Joshu who spoke to his assembly, saying, "The real Way is not difficult. It only abhors choice and attachment. With but a single word there may arise choice and attachment or there may arise clarity. This old monk does not have that clarity. Do you appreciate the meaning of this or not?" Then a monk asked, "If you do not have that clarity, what do you appreciate?" Joshu said, "I do not know that, either." The monk said, "If you do not know, how can you say you do not have that clarity?" Joshu said, "Asking the question is good enough. Now make your bows and retire."[1]

Here Joshu says that the real Way is not difficult, but this is only true when you stop picking and choosing. If you want to follow the example of Joshu, just cease being attached to likes and dislikes; otherwise the perfect Way is going to be difficult and hard to accomplish. Ask yourself first: what is the Way? If you are unable to answer this question and have been studying for some years, you should penetrate to the heart of the matter and take your understanding to a teacher who can discern the depth of your realization. To have only an intellectual or conceptual idea about what the Way is will not suffice; you would still be mountains and rivers away from it. If you can't demonstrate with your whole being this Way in face-to-face confrontation with a true master, your Zen eye may be only partially open.

Next, you must know what Joshu means by "not difficult." Joshu's "not difficult" goes far beyond any deluded understanding of difficult and easy. Joshu's "not difficult" is that of someone who has dropped attachment to life and death. Maybe you still care too much whether you are alive or dead, enlightened or deluded, good or bad, right or wrong.

Now, what is meant by "the perfect Way abhors choice and attachment"? Are you still picking and choosing? Do you still hold preferences for and against people and things? Are you still attached to the company of those you love and want to get rid of those you despise? If so, for you the perfect Way is difficult. Do you crave and seek after liberation and want to get rid of your attachments and fetters? If so, you are not free like Master Joshu.

Joshu has no clarity, so he is not attached to clarity. Do you appreciate the brilliance of this? Are you hanging on to your little glimpses into reality? If so, why not aspire, like Joshu, to go far beyond such things? If you are not walking in the same sandals as Joshu, then you have not yet truly awakened.

The monk in this case could not appreciate the depth and clarity of old Joshu, so he asked him, "If you do not have that clarity, what do you appreciate?" At this point Joshu shows his heart, gall bladder, and spleen and tells the monk, "I do not know that, either."

When you say, "I don't know," is it the "I don't know!" of Joshu or is it the not-knowing of this poor monk? How confident are you in your not-knowing? If you are not seeing with the same eyes as Joshu, then you need to work much harder to penetrate into this vital matter.

Finally, Joshu loses patience with this deluded monk and reveals his true compassion. He tells him to make his bows and get out, to stop wasting his time with such nonsense.

Master Engo prepared an introduction to this koan:

> The universe is too narrow; the sun, moon, and stars are all at once darkened. Even if blows from the stick fall like raindrops and the "katsu" shouts sound like thunder, you are still far short of the truth of Buddhism. Even the Buddhas of the three worlds can only nod to themselves, and the Patriarchs of all ages do not exhaustively demonstrate its profundity. The whole treasury of sutras is inadequate to expound its deep meaning. Even the clearest-eyed failed to save themselves. At this point, how do you conduct yourself? Mentioning the name of the Buddha is like trudging through the mire. To utter the word "Zen" is to cover your face with shame. Not only those who have long practiced Zen but beginners, too, should exert themselves to attain directly to the secret.[2]

If you have been practicing Zen for many years and have not yet penetrated to the essence of "the real Way is not difficult," you cannot even free yourself from a stone grave that is locked from the outside. How do you expect to liberate sentient beings? With your pitiful concerns about right and wrong, good and evil, you're not even worthy to be called a student of the Way, let alone a master of Zen! You should get yourself to a monastery and practice under a true master so you can swing your arms freely and move your legs without hindrance. You must be able to discern clearly the true Way from the false, Buddhas from deluded people.

It is impossible to sever the source of transmigration without casting away the delusive mind. In the same way, if a king fails to heed the advice of his retainers, virtuous policy will not prevail, and he will be unable to govern the country well.

If you have not cut the root of dualistic mind completely, then you will go on transmigrating through the six realms and the three worlds eternally. You will be like a hungry ghost who is creeping around from here to there, searching for the Truth but unable to swallow it. Your belly will be unsatisfied, your thirst will be unquenchable, and your head will be filled with notions of right and wrong, good and evil. You will look to real masters with envy and jealousy and not know why you feel so miserable and vulnerable. It is only because you have not taken care of the great matter of life and death and still have uncertainty about who you are and where you are going.

If you really want to know what you are and where you come from, you must find an accomplished master to study with and go to the source of the matter, relinquishing everything that you have and becoming, truly, the person who stands alone on top of Mount Sumeru.[3] Then you must drop to the very depths of hell where you walk freely with the homeless, begging for your food and accepting whatever pittance is offered to you.

Emperor Wu of Liang asked Bodhidharma, "What is the first principle of the holy teaching?" Bodhidharma said, "Vast emptiness, nothing holy." The Emperor said, "Who is this person confronting me?" Bodhidharma said, "I do not know." The emperor did not grasp his meaning. Bodhidharma then crossed the river and went on to the land of Wei.[4]

Emperor Wu had not yet realized the primary principle

of the true Dharma, so he had to ask the great Bodhidharma what it was. The Master, holding nothing back, revealed the Truth: "Vast emptiness. No holiness." How do you understand this first principle of Zen? Do you understand it merely conceptually or have you become truly one with these words? Are you completely empty of yourself and no longer holy? Or are you still full of yourself and carrying the stink of Zen? Are you still seeking or have you really found?

If you have found anything whatsoever, even so much as a speck of dust, you are deluded and beyond help. If you are a young Zen novice, find yourself a good teacher and penetrate to the heart of this matter. If you are a senior Zen practitioner and still have doubt and uncertainty, take out Manjusri's sword and cut off your own head, or hand that sword to an accomplished swordsman and beg him to mercifully do the job for you. If you still see so much as a particle apart from yourself, you must cut off all discriminating thoughts.

We must mourn for the state of affairs of Zen today, for so few have truly realized Bodhidharma's profound meaning. How many can answer the question, "Why did Bodhidharma come from the West?" If you have any feeling of being special, holding on to any position or integrity, still having a shred of decency left, you cannot even save your own self. You will be lost forever in the hell realm. Only after you have given up everything, even your pride and dignity, are you worthy to be called a true Zen monk. If you are still holding on to fame, name, position, or money, then you are still looking out from your prison window, trying to lead others to freedom. You haven't even so much as sniffed the fresh air of true liberation or smelled the sweet fragrance of the old barbarian!

If you know Bodhidharma intimately, why has the Western barbarian no beard? If you think it's because he shaved this morning or he is a female, you are gravely mistaken. A monk once asked Ummon, "What will it be when trees wither and leaves fall?" Ummon answered, "You embody the golden breeze."[5] What is the golden breeze that you embody? How would you manifest it? These questions and your presentations must be put forth before a master who has thoroughly penetrated these koans himself. Without this dynamic exchange, true Zen will die. It will become so feeble that even the spineless can practice it.

How do you understand Bodhidharma's "I do not know"? His not-knowing is the not-knowing of "I don't know!" This is the not-knowing of someone who has searched for the meaning of life and death to the very depths of the sea and to the far corners of the universe, leaving no stone or blade of grass unturned, and without a shadow of a doubt has realized the meaning of Bodhidharma coming from the West. Only Bodhidharma can know his meaning. If you don't shave with the same razor and sit in the same cave, you are not yet truly enlightened, let alone ready to lead others to liberation. Those who try to do so only deceive themselves and those poor unfortunate souls who cannot discern good from bad and have never met a true man of no rank.

After Bodhidharma had departed, Emperor Wu took up the matter with Shiko. Shiko said, "Does your majesty know that person yet?" The emperor said, "I don't know him." Shiko said, "That was the Bodhisattva Kannon conveying the mind-seal of the Buddha." The emperor felt regretful, and at once sought to have a messenger dispatched to urge him to return. Shiko said, "There is no use in sending a messenger. Even if everyone in the country went after him, he would not return."[6]

Have you, like Emperor Wu of Liang, missed your opportunity to truly meet the old barbarian? If you have had the opportunity and did not manage to swallow this bearded one in a single gulp, you will flail around in the sea of confusion for lifetimes. Bodhidharma will never come back, and if you want to get to the Truth, you must cross the great river, chase after him, and swallow your pride. If there is anything left of your dignity and composure, your ideas of right and wrong, you will never see him face-to-face again.

Master Engo says: "Smoke over the hill indicates fire, horns over the fence indicate an ox. Given one corner, you grasp the other three; one glance, and you discern the smallest difference. Such quickness, however, is only too common among patch-robed monks. When you have stopped the deluded activity of consciousness, then, whatever situation you may find yourself in, you enjoy perfect freedom, in adversity and prosperity, in taking and giving. Now tell me, how in fact will this sort of person behave?"[7]

Notes

[1] *Hekiganroku*, Case 2, Main Subject, in Sekida, 149–50.
[2] Dogen Zenji, *Shobogenzo,* "Bendowa," translated by Nishiyama, Volume One, 147.
[3] Mount Sumeru: the "world mountain" of ancient Indian cosmology, the dwelling place of the gods that stands at the center of the universe.
[4] *Hekiganroku*, Case 1, Main Subject, in Sekida, 147.
[5] *Hekiganroku*, Case 27, Main Subject, in Sekida, 218.
[6] *Hekiganroku*, Case 1, Main Subject, in Sekida, 147.
[7] *Hekiganroku*, Case 1, Master Engo's Introduction in Sekida, 147.

Points to Watch in Practicing the Way
Point Three

The Need to Realize the Way
Through Constant Training

Lay people believe that government office can be acquired as a result of study. The Buddha Shakyamuni teaches, however, that training encompasses enlightenment. I have never heard of anyone who became a government official without study or realized enlightenment without training.

No one has ever realized true enlightenment without practice. Many have had some kind of opening or mystical experience, but it is not the same caliber as what the Buddha Shakyamuni is speaking about. Enlightenment embraces training. The history of Zen records countless cases of those who had to go through tremendous hardship in order to attain true realization. It is Shakyamuni Buddha's teaching that training encompasses enlightenment. There is no enlightenment apart from training. Practice is enlightenment, enlightenment is practice.

How, then, does training imply enlightenment? Training is realization and only through training is your true nature expressed in everyday life. It is a very subtle point, impossible to grasp fully unless one has had direct experience of this. It reveals that whatever you do from morning until night is the manifestation of your true nature.

The problem is that there are people who, after having some glimpse of enlightenment, draw premature conclusions. They believe that, since enlightenment is nothing but one's life, after realization everything can be called Zen practice and it no longer matters how much they practice zazen. What may originally have been a genuine realization becomes a big delusion and simply a way to justify oneself.

In the *Fukanzazengi*, Dogen Zenji said:

> The Way is basically perfect and all-pervading. How could it be contingent upon practice and realization? The Dharma-vehicle is free and untrammelled. What need is there for man's concentrated effort? Indeed, the whole body is far beyond the world's dust. Who could believe in a means to brush it clean? It is never apart from right where one is. What is the use of going off here and there to practice?
>
> And yet, if there is the slightest discrepancy, the Way is as distant as heaven from earth. If the least like or dislike arises, the Mind is lost in confusion. Suppose one gains pride of understanding and inflates one's own enlightenment, glimpsing the Wisdom that runs through all things, attaining the Way and, clarifying the Mind, raising an aspiration to escalate the very sky. One is making the initial, partial excursions about the frontiers but is still somewhat deficient in the vital Way of total emancipation.

Need I mention the Buddha, who was possessed of inborn knowledge?—The influence of his six years of upright sitting is noticeable still. Or Bodhidharma's transmission of the mind-seal? The fame of his nine years of wall-sitting is celebrated to this day. Since this was the case with the saints of old, how can men of today dispense with negotiation of the Way? You should therefore cease from practice based on intellectual understanding, pursuing words and following after speech, and learn the backward step that turns your light inwardly to illuminate yourself. Body and mind of themselves will drop away, and your original face will be manifest. If you want to attain suchness, you should practice suchness without delay.[1]

Without zazen it is a mistake to think that you are practicing Zen, for in actuality you are not. If you really want to accomplish the Buddha Way, many years of hard training are necessary. With practice there is realization; with realization there is actualization. Without practice there is no realization; without realization there is no actualization.

Only long and intensive training makes it possible to grasp the fact that Zen includes everything you do from morning until night. But whatever insight or *kensho* you may have had, if you stop doing zazen or don't sit enough, you're sure to get obstructed by your realization. Your understanding will only harden as time goes by, crystallizing into something solid. The life you live will then be based on a concept of reality rather than reality itself, and your idea of training will become merely trying to live up to your concept. You will watch yourself carefully to behave in accord with your picture of what you believe Zen practice should look like. This may appear to you as training, but it is just another idea. The greater the realization the greater the chance of getting attached to it, so the only choice is endless practice.

It is easier to bring people to enlightenment than it is to help them cast it away. The simple fact is that before enlightenment no one is really happy with the way they are; only realization makes us feel totally fulfilled. No wonder there is resistance to letting go of enlightenment. We're bound to feel insufficient again, realizing how much further there is to go. It may feel like we are losing something and sliding backwards, but this is supposed to happen; it is part of the process. There is the analogy of ascending the mountain. Once you reach the summit you must descend again into the muddy water, back into the world of delusion. You cannot remain on top of the mountain forever.

Kyosho asked a monk, "What is that sound outside?" "The sound of raindrops," replied the monk. Kyosho said, "Ordinary people are upside down, falling into delusion about themselves, and pursuing outside objects." "What about yourself, Your Reverence?" asked the monk. Kyosho said, "I am on the brink of falling into delusion about myself." The monk asked, "What do you mean, 'on the brink of falling into delusion about yourself'?" Kyosho said, "To attain the world of emptiness may not be so difficult, but to express the bare substance is hard."[2]

What does it mean, "I am on the brink of falling into delusion about myself"? To see what Master Kyosho is saying, first you have to go beyond enlightenment and delusion, then, taking a further step for the sake of all sentient beings, go back into the muddy water of delusion. What is "the world of emptiness"? And how do you express "the bare substance"? If you recognize so much as a speck of enlightenment, you are already beyond help.

Although it is true that different training methods exist—those based on faith or the Law—the sudden or gradual realization of enlightenment—still one realizes enlightenment as a result of training. In the same way, although the depth of people's learning differs, as does their speed of comprehension, government office is acquired through accumulated study. None of these things depends on whether the rulers are superior or not, or whether one's luck is good or bad.

Realization always appears suddenly, but it does not happen by accident. One has to be ripe for the Truth, and that takes years of diligent practice. Then to clarify this realization involves an ongoing process of refining one's life. So a sudden and a gradual aspect of training can be distinguished. Some Buddhist schools and teachers concentrate more on the first aspect, others more on the second; still, enlightenment is only realized through practice. There is no other way. All the great masters had to go through severe and difficult training to be worthy to be called a Patriarch of Zen.

No matter what path you follow, the gradual or the sudden, training and realization are always connected. One does not go without the other, and yet in some schools the importance of realization has been lost almost completely. People sit for years like stone Buddhas without ever waking up. In other schools the opposite has happened: enlightenment has become just a goal to be attained, and students quit practicing as soon as they have some realization. Dogen Zenji shows us both sides of the truth. Through practice there is enlightenment, and practice itself is the enlightenment. It sounds contradictory, but it is not. The very first time you do zazen you are a sitting Buddha, but it may take you many long years of sitting to realize this fact.

Rinzai devoted himself to zazen exclusively for six years before he was persuaded to go face-to-face with Master Obaku in his private chambers. Not knowing what to say, he was told by the head monk, Bokushu, to ask the Master, "What is the clearly manifested essence of the Buddha-dharma?" Rinzai, after making his appropriate bows, put the question to the great Obaku. Obaku then mercilessly beat Rinzai with his stick. Rinzai stumbled out, confused and bewildered, and asked Bokushu, "Where was my fault?" Bokushu said, "The old man must not have understood your question properly. Go back and ask him a second time." Rinzai returned to the lion's cave, only to be beaten by Obaku again. Now he came out crying and whimpering, "Why is he beating me like this?" Bokushu again said, "Obaku must be really confused. Go and ask him a third time, 'What is the meaning of Zen?'" So for a third time, this helpless young monk entered the *dokusan* room of the master. Obaku showed no mercy and he beat this retarded fellow to the bones.

Now Rinzai was really angry! He went out and told Bokushu, "I am leaving this monastery forever. The old man in there is completely mad. He is not a compassionate Zen master!" Bokushu begged Rinzai to have the courtesy to let the old man know that he was taking leave of the monastery. So for a fourth time, Rinzai entered the cave of poison grass and informed Obaku of his intentions. This time Obaku said, "If it must be so, then I encourage you to go and see my Dharma brother, Daigu."

Rinzai went to Daigu's place, related the incident with Obaku, and beseeched Daigu, "Where was my error?" Daigu said, "Obaku is too grandmotherly kind; he completely exhausted himself for your sake. Then you come here and ask me where you were in error." At this, Rinzai had a great enlightenment and exclaimed, "Now I know that Obaku's Zen is not much at all." Daigu grabbed hold of him and said, "A moment ago you asked where you were in error, and now you say that Obaku's Zen is not much at all!" Rinzai punched Daigu three times in the ribs, knocking him down. Daigu got up, shoved Rinzai away, and said, "Your teacher is Obaku." Rinzai then returned to Obaku's monastery, where he eventually succeeded the Dharma.[3]

This is the spirit of Rinzai Zen, but there are hardly any masters today with the compassion of Obaku, nor are there many students with the determination and guts of Rinzai. What kind of Zen is being transmitted these days? Is it so watered down that it has lost its unique flavor? Will we be able in the years to come to distinguish Zen from psychotherapy? If a psychiatrist were to treat a patient the way Obaku treated Rinzai, he would be charged with abusive behavior and kicked out of the profession. In our world today, everyone is worried about losing their license to practice or being sued by their clients or students. Did Rinzai run to his attorney and threaten to file suit against Obaku? Did Daigu tell Rinzai that he was a victim of abuse? No, only that Obaku had been too grandmotherly kind to him!

In this day and age there are those who have never enjoyed the beating at the hands of their master's blind stick and speak wantonly about how teachers should not abuse their students. They know absolutely nothing about the transmission of the true Buddha-dharma, which goes beyond killing and not killing, beyond enlightened and ordinary beings. These people are only binding themselves without the use of a rope to rules and regulations that don't apply to true

Zen. They should go back into psychotherapy, work on their relationship with their parents, and leave Zen to those who have blood in their veins and bones in their body. Are you feeling abused by now? If not, see the following.

When Ummon was desperately seeking the Way, he went to great Master Bokushu. At this time Bokushu had received the seal of approval from Obaku and was holed up in a hut deep in the mountains. Ummon had to cross a river to get to Bokushu's hut. When he pounded on the great wooden door, Bokushu cried out, "Who is there?" Ummon answered in a feeble voice, "It is me, monk Ummon." Seven-foot Bokushu threw open the door, towering over the five-foot Ummon. Grabbing him and lifting him several feet off the ground, Bokushu shouted, "Say a word of Zen! Quickly! Quickly!" Ummon couldn't open his mouth to save himself. Thrown out by force, he retreated to the other side of the river to lick his wounds.

The next day he mustered up enough courage to once more request the teaching from Bokushu. Again he knocked on the door and Bokushu bellowed, "Who's there?" "It is me, Monk Ummon." Once more the giant opened the door and grabbed Ummon by the collar, shouting, "Say a word of Zen! Quickly! Quickly!" Once more Ummon was flustered and speechless. Bokushu tossed him out and slammed the door. This time Ummon stayed up all night, sitting in zazen, wondering where he was at fault. Why was he being so abused?

The next morning he decided to try once again. With his pride in hand, he once again knocked on the great wooden door of Bokushu's hut. This time, however, he had a scheme: he thought to himself, "When he grabs me, I will clutch the pillar by the door and he won't be able to throw me out." When Bokushu tossed him out for the third time, Ummon held onto the pillar, but his leg got caught in the door as it slammed and was crushed. He cried out in agony and in that moment experienced great enlightenment.[4]

If you have never experienced the pain of Ummon, you cannot be said to know what Zen is all about. If your leg has not been crushed or your neck choked, or you have not known the blows of your master's stick, you are like a ghost haunting the trees and bushes. You don't know the great joy of being completely destroyed by your teacher and the great liberation that accompanies it.

There are those who would like to make Zen safe and secure and palatable to our society. How could the kind of behavior these two great masters displayed ever be justified? When you read about it in a book, you may laugh and praise their compassion, but when similar things happen to you or to people you know, it is hard to appreciate such action. Real masters run the risk of being kicked out of their lineage and sent to prison, or at least to a psychiatric ward, charged with abuse and deemed unworthy of wearing Buddhist robes.

Teaching that appears abusive may take various forms other than physical beating. Consider the following stories from the Tibetan Buddhist tradition. When Marpa was seeking to resume his studies with Naropa, he brought an offering of gold dust with him on the journey to India. According to Chogyam Trungpa Rinpoche:

> Naropa seemed very cold and impersonal, almost hostile, and his first words to Marpa were, "Good to see you again. How much gold have you for my teachings?" Marpa had brought a large amount of gold but wanted to save some for his expenses and the trip home, so he

opened his pack and gave Naropa only a portion of what he had. Naropa looked at the offering and said, "No, this is not enough. I need more gold than this for my teaching. Give me all your gold." Marpa gave him a bit more and still Naropa demanded all, and this went on until finally Naropa laughed and said, "Do you think you can buy my teaching with your deception?" At this point Marpa yielded and gave Naropa all the gold he had. To his shock, Naropa picked up the bags and began flinging the gold dust in the air.

Suddenly Marpa felt extremely confused and paranoid. He could not understand what was happening. He had worked hard for the gold to buy the teaching he so wanted. Naropa had seemed to indicate that he needed the gold and would teach Marpa in return for it. Yet he was throwing it away! Then Naropa said to him, "What need have I of gold? The whole world is gold for me!" This was a great moment of opening for Marpa.[5]

In Milarepa's case, the situation developed quite differently. He was a peasant, much less learned and sophisticated than Marpa had been when he met Naropa, and he had committed many crimes, including murder. He was miserably unhappy, yearned for enlightenment, and was willing to pay any price that Marpa might ask. So Marpa had Milarepa pay on a very literal physical level. He had him build a series of houses for him, one after the other, and after each was completed Marpa would tell Milarepa to tear the house down and put all the stones back where he had found them, so as not to mar the landscape. Each time Marpa ordered Milarepa to dismantle a house, he would give some absurd excuse, such as having been drunk when he ordered the house built or never having ordered such a house in the first place. And each time Milarepa, full of longing for the teachings, would tear the house down and start again.

Finally Marpa designed a tower with nine stories. Milarepa suffered terrific physical hardship in carrying the stones and building the house and, when he had finished, he went to Marpa and once more asked for the teachings. But Marpa said to him, "You want to receive teachings from me, just like that, merely because you built this tower for me? Well, I'm afraid you will still have to give me a gift as an initiation fee."

By this time Milarepa had no possessions left whatsoever, having spent all his time and labor building towers. But Damema, Marpa's wife, felt sorry for him and said, "These towers you have built are such a wonderful gesture of devotion and faith. Surely my husband won't mind if I give you some sacks of barley and a roll of cloth for your initiation fee." So Milarepa took the barley and cloth to the initiation circle where Marpa was teaching and offered them as his fee, along with the gifts of the other students. But Marpa, when he recognized the gift, was furious and shouted at Milarepa, "These things belong to me, you hypocrite! You try to deceive me!" And he literally kicked Milarepa out of the initiation circle.

At this point Milarepa gave up all hope of ever getting Marpa to give him the teachings. In despair, he decided to commit suicide and was just about to kill himself when Marpa came to him and told him that he was ready to receive the teaching.[6]

35

How far your Zen eye has opened depends on your capacity and faith to go through severe training. Some will grasp the truth in an instant, others will fumble about for decades, but all who persevere with their whole heart can enter the gate of liberation. Do not stop somewhere along the way.

The only thing that keeps you from fully accomplishing the Way and realizing complete enlightenment is your half-hearted desire to do so. If you have not yet raised the Bodhi-mind to seek the Way and liberate all sentient beings, you should do so at once. One thing is for sure: enlightenment only occurs as a result of true practice. It does not depend on either luck or chance, only on the sincerity of your determination and effort. If you do not succeed in liberating yourself, it is not the fault of your teacher, but your inability to give yourself completely to the Way.

What are you still clinging to? Is it to a feeling of security and identity, or is it to your fear of total relinquishment? Do you want to go on transmigrating in the three worlds forever, never putting an end to the suffering you cause yourself and others?

If government office could be acquired without study, who could transmit the method by which the former king successfully ruled the nation? If enlightenment could be realized without training, who could understand the teaching of the Tathagata, distinguishing, as it does, the difference between delusion and enlightenment? Understand that although you train in the world of delusion, enlightenment is already there. Then, for the first time, you will realize that boats and rafts [the sutras] are but yesterday's dream and will be able to sever forever the old views that bound you to them.

The teaching of the Tathagata clarifies the difference between delusion and enlightenment. It is only because of dualistic understanding that you are unable to discern the true from the false. You think that enlightenment is something to be attained and that delusion is something to get rid of. You don't know yet that delusion is enlightenment and enlightenment is delusion. In the midst of delusion you are already the enlightened one, the Buddha. Realizing enlightenment, you are deluded. How to go far beyond both enlightenment and delusion and walk hand-in-hand with the Buddhas and Patriarchs? Old Joshu was no longer concerned about such things. Bodhidharma couldn't even remember the meaning of either enlightenment or delusion. Should the Buddha appear in front of you, just kill him. Why are you trying to be so kind and sweet? It is only through such misguided ideas that we destroy the life of the Patriarchs.

Having truly attained enlightenment, you will realize that all the sutras and shastras are but painted cakes which cannot satisfy your real hunger. They are only illusions, and if you hang on to them you can never sever your views about good and evil, right and wrong. Without real practice you will not be able to drop all your preconceived notions and dualistic understanding. Being well versed in the sutras, while being ignorant of the true practice of zazen, only stands as a barrier to true liberation.

You must forget all you know before you can enter the gateless gate of Zen. If you have not entered this gate under the guidance of a true master who himself has accomplished the Way, you should, like the great masters of old who realized their insufficiency, seek out a true master. It is only through a genuine teacher that your understanding can be tested. If it is not, you may go on believing for decades that

37

you understand what *mu* is. Even if you understand *mu*, do you really know the source? Can you pass through Hakuin's Sound of One Hand? And do you know how to cut the One Hand in two? Even if you can pass through these initial koans for beginners, do you know the last word of Zen? If you think that the last word is a word or is not a word, you are gravely mistaken. If you know the last word of Zen, then you still have to realize what the great Ganto whispered to old Tokusan. Consider the following:

> Tokusan one day came down to the dining room carrying his bowls. Seppo said, "Old Master, the bell has not rung and the drum has not yet been struck. Where are you going with your bowls?" Tokusan at once turned back to his room. Seppo told this incident to Ganto, who remarked, "Great Master though he is, Tokusan has not yet grasped the last word of Zen." Hearing of it, Tokusan sent his attendant to call Ganto in, and asked, "Do you not approve of me?" Ganto whispered his reply to him. Tokusan was satisfied and silent. The next day Tokusan appeared on the rostrum. Sure enough, his talk was different from the usual ones. Ganto came in front of the monastery, laughed heartily, clapping his hands, and said, "What a great joy it is! The old Master has now grasped the last word of Zen. From now on nobody in the world can ever make light of him."[7]

By memorizing the sutras and studying the shastras, you will only keep yourself bound by intellectual and conceptual understanding. If you come face-to-face with a true master with your pride in your hand, you will not even be able to pass a single koan. Don't you want to be completely free and unfettered? Don't you want to know the great joy and peace of being liberated from suffering and confusion? Only through your own efforts and sincere practice can you truly attain the Way. Not even a Buddha can force it upon you: a horse can be led to water but cannot be made to drink.

The Buddha does not force this understanding on you.
Rather, it comes naturally from your training in the Way, for train-
ing invites enlightenment. Your own treasure does not come from the
outside. Since enlightenment is one with training, enlightened action
leaves no traces. Therefore, when looking back on training with
enlightened eyes, you will find there is no illusion to be seen, just as
white clouds extending for ten thousand ri *cover the whole sky.*

Training invites enlightenment. Realization only comes when the time and situation are ripe. You have to become like the chick inside the egg, ready to peck from the inside. If the master is not close by at the critical moment, you will succumb in your efforts. This is why it is essential to become intimate with your teacher.

A monk once asked Master Kyosei, "I am pecking from inside. I beg you, master, please peck from the outside." Kyosei said, "But will you be alive?" The monk said, "I am living vigorously like this! If I were not alive, I would be laughed at." Kyosei said, "You, a half-baked fellow!"[8]

The question is, how do you prepare yourself for such a moment? Only by going to the depth of despair, having lost everything you hold dear. Then and only then, through the benevolent compassion of your teacher, can the final blow be struck. But if you are like this unfortunate monk, thinking that you are ready for such compassion, you'd better look again. If you are only half-baked, the blow will come prema-turely, and you will surely die of sudden exposure. If you are too distant from your teacher when the right time comes, how do you expect his stick to reach you? You will certainly rot in the shell for all eternity!

Your own treasure does not come from the outside but is innate. At the time of your birth, you were born only with the One Buddha-mind, which is unborn and undying from the beginning. You received nothing else at your birth but this wonderful Buddha treasure. Why do you need to seek after enlightenment when there is not even so much as a speck of delusion to be found within you?

No one can give you more than you already have. What is it that you think you are lacking? Since enlightenment is one with training, the action of the enlightened one leaves no trace, as a bird that flies in the sky leaves no mark. After great enlightenment you will realize that all efforts were finally in vain, that from the beginning there was no delusion to be cast away and no enlightenment to be gained. Delusion is enlightenment, and in the midst of your delusion you practice the Buddha Way.

When enlightenment is harmonized with training, you cannot step on even a single particle of dust. Should you be able to do so, you will be as far removed from enlightenment as heaven is from earth. If you return to your true Self, you can transcend even the status of the Buddha.

When enlightenment and practice are one, you will not recognize so much as a speck of dust apart from yourself. From the beginning there has never been such a thing as delusion, so what enlightenment could be attained? When you have truly harmonized enlightenment and practice, you cannot step on even a single particle of dirt. If you could find so much as a speck of delusion within, you would be so far from enlightenment that even all the Buddhas and Tathagatas would be unable to rescue you.

When you realize your true face before your parents were born you go far beyond enlightenment and delusion, Buddha and sentient being, sanity and madness. If you would just be your ordinary self, with nothing further to seek after, just pissing and shitting when nature calls, you would go far beyond even the status of the Buddha Shakyamuni.

Notes

[1] Dogen Zenji, *Fukanzazengi*, translated by Norman Waddell and Abe Masao in *Eastern Buddhist*, Vol. vi/2, 1973, 121–22.

[2] *Hekiganroku*, Case 46, translated by Yamada Koun and Robert Aitken (unpublished).

[3] Adapted from Sekida, 177–78.

[4] Sekida, 294.

[5] Trungpa, 36–37.

[6] Trungpa, 37–38.

[7] *Mumonkan*, Case 13, in Shibayama, 101.

[8] *Hekiganroku*, Case 16, translated by Yamada Koun and Robert Aitken (unpublished).

Points to Watch in Practicing the Way
Point Four

The Need for Selfless Practice of the Way

In the practice of the Way it is necessary to accept the true teachings of our predecessors, setting aside our own preconceived notions. The Way cannot be realized with mind or without it. Unless the mind of constant practice is one with the Way, neither body nor mind will know peace. When the body and mind are not at peace, they become obstacles to enlightenment.

If you wish to practice the Way, it is absolutely essential to accept the true teachings of the ancient Zen masters, dropping all your preconceptions. The Buddha Way cannot be realized with mind. Whatever comes up with the mind will always be concepts, lifeless, lacking the true spirit and freedom of Zen. The Way cannot be realized without mind either, for without mind there would be mere blankness. You must go beyond mind and not-mind and realize the True Mind. If you go forward, you miss it. If you regress, you will be far from the Way. What will you do? Bodhidharma demanded of

43

Eka, "Bring me your mind!" What mind? And how will you present it to the old barbarian? If you cannot do so, you will lose your life and your ancestors will have died in vain. Now tell me, where is this Mind?

Unless the mind of constant practice is one with the Way, neither body nor mind will know true peace. When the body and mind are not at peace, it is impossible for you to attain enlightenment. It is only through the practice of *jijuyu-zanmai*, self-fulfilling *samadhi*, that mind and body will know true peace. Even though it is innately present in everyone, unless you practice, it cannot be manifested and unless there is realization it cannot be perceived. By this *samadhi* alone, you find true reality and attain perfect harmony; just cease from discriminating. It is only through this *samadhi* that self-less practice continues and the true transmission is revealed. Dogen Zenji said:

> All the Buddhas and Patriarchs who have realized the Buddha-dharma insist that proper sitting in this *samadhi* is the way to attain enlightenment. All the ancients who attained enlightenment followed this practice. The transmission from teacher to student is based upon the reception and preservation of this *samadhi*. That transmission is the ultimate Buddha-dharma. From the very beginning of your study with a true master, it is not necessary to burn incense, make prostrations, practice penances, or study the sutras—just let body and mind drop off! Even a single sitting in this *jijuyu samadhi* the Buddha-mind seal is imprinted in your body, mind, and words; simultaneously, the entire Dharma world is also imprinted with the Buddha-mind seal—all space is enlightenment. The Buddhas' enlightened joy increases

and their wonderful attributes renew themselves. Furthermore, all beings in the ten directions of the universe are pure and bright in body and mind; they realize perfect liberation and reveal their original body as the Buddha. That is, all dharmas themselves are Buddha's enlightenment—his body, his sitting under the bodhi tree, his turning of the wheel of the Dharma; all dharmas are expounding the most profound and subtle form of *prajna* wisdom. Moreover, since awakened ones have the ability to transfer their merit, people who sit in zazen share in the truth acquired by Buddha, casting off body and mind and all worldly attachments. Their Wisdom permeates even the tiniest speck of dust and it cultivates, perfects, and develops Buddhahood and each Dharma.[1]

According to Master Rinzai:

There are certain shaved monks who tell their students that the Buddha is the ultimate and that he only accomplished the Way by bringing to complete maturity the practices cultivated during three great world ages. Followers of the Way, if you say the Buddha is the ultimate, how does it come that at the age of eighty he died lying on his side between the twin trees at the town of Kushinagara? The Buddha, where is he now? It is clear that like you and me he lived and died and so is not different from us. You say that the thirty-two marks and the eighty characteristics distinguish the Buddha. But then the mighty sage who turned the wheel of the Dharma should also have been a Tathagata. Clearly all this is just fantasy and illusion."[2]

How are constant practice and the Way to be harmonized?
To do so the mind must neither be attached to nor reject anything;
it must be completely free from attachment to fame and profit. One
does not undergo Buddhist training in order to gain a good reputa-
tion. The minds of Buddhist trainees, like those of most people these
days, however, are far from understanding the Way. They do that
which others praise, even though they know it to be false. On the
other hand, they do not practice that which others scorn, even
though they know it to be the true Way. How regrettable!

When the mind is dropped in zazen, the Way is manifested; only then will body and mind know true peace. When
body and mind are not at peace, then they become obstacles
to realization.

How to harmonize practice and the Way? The key is to
hold no preference: neither be attached to nor reject anything.
For a long time students can do nothing but make an attempt
to practice true zazen. They need a goal in order to begin, and
yet this very goal creates the illusion of separation and makes
it impossible to be in harmony with the Way. It takes most
students many years of sincere training to drop this illusion
and be one with the Way.

Dogen Zenji lost his mother when he was only eight. He
had his first insight into the transiency of life when he saw the
smoke of incense rising at her funeral. Becoming a monk at
thirteen, still he had to go through tremendous hardship,
traveling to China, almost dying on the way. After some years
of searching there, finally body and mind dropped off and
true peace was found.

One does not undergo Buddhist training in order to
gain a good reputation. That is not the point. If you are practicing for this reason, you are far off the mark. If you do that
which others praise, even knowing it to be false, and you do

not practice that which others scorn, knowing it to be the true Way, then you are completely mistaken.

What is it that most people practice in order to be praised and what is it that they avoid practicing in order not to be condemned? They practice that which conforms to the standards of their culture. They avoid doing anything that goes against what society sees as acceptable. Our society, with its strong work ethic, regards complete relinquishment as unacceptable. To leave home, country, family, profession, and position in order to pursue single-mindedly the practice of zazen is unthinkable, even for some who teach Zen. Conditioning about what is right and wrong is that strong!

What is lacking is true faith in the Way. Therefore independence is cherished; surrender is scorned. Most people today see independence as a virtue, and therefore good. This is not to say that independence is bad and dependence is good; it's just that in order to truly accomplish the Way of the Buddhas and the Patriarchs, you have to go through dependency. This is the point. Anyone who wants to taste true liberation has to go through the difficult process of submission.

This process is misunderstood in our time. People would rather avoid the pain of surrender by meeting the teacher on an equal level, like a good friend or even a buddy; but it does not work this way. If you really wish to receive the true Dharma, you have to let go of all your conventional ideas about enlightened teachers.

To quote a modern Tibetan Buddhist teacher, the late Jamgon Kongtrul: "Do not find fault with the guru. How can a Buddha have faults? Whatever he does, let him do it! Even if you see your guru having sexual relations, telling lies and so on, calmly meditate as follows: 'These are my guru's unsurpassed skillful methods of training disciples. Through these methods he has brought many sentient beings to spiritual maturity and liberation. This is a hundred, a thousand times more wonderful than preserving a pure moral code! This is not deception or hypocrisy but the highest mode of conduct!'"[3]

Of course, to follow Jamgon Kongtrul's advice, you must be sure that you are working with a true teacher, one who has gone through the whole process of submission to a master himself and who has harmonized practice and the Way. There are teachers who, having not gone through complete surrender themselves, are afraid of the responsibility for their students' submission. Only a Buddha can transmit to a Buddha. An ordinary person cannot transmit the true Dharma to an ordinary person.

Master Rinzai:

> There are everywhere teachers who do not distinguish the false from the true. When students come to question them on Bodhi, on nirvana, on the Trikaya, or on objective wisdom, the blind teacher at once begins to explain them verbosely to the student. And if the student abuses him, he takes his stick and rudely beats the student. Such a teacher has neither eye nor manners. Do not hope for anything from him.

> There is still another lot of blind old rascals who do not know good from bad. They point to the east and indicate the west, they like fine weather and fancy rain, like stone lanterns and uncarved pillars. Look—have they any eyebrows left? If the students do not know that "all are supplied with concurrent causes," their hearts become infatuated. Teachers like this are all like wild fox sprites or demons. But the good student gives a

deep chuckle and merely says: "Blind old fools, beguiling the people."[4]

Reflect quietly on whether your mind and actions are one with the Buddha-dharma or not. If you do so, you will realize how shameful they are. The penetrating eyes of the Buddhas and Patriarchs are constantly illuminating the entire universe.

Reflecting honestly on whether one's mind and actions are truly in accord with the Buddha-dharma is often a very humbling experience. The deluded love to feel good about themselves because they are attached to self. The awakened have dropped the self and realize how shameful their actions are. Who is not continuously defiling the precepts: slandering, blaming, and speaking ill of others without even realizing it; elevating oneself by putting others down; blaming others in order to avoid taking responsibility; hurting people, friends and foes alike? We are not bad people because of this, only human. When we practice, we realize that we are no better than anyone else; but we are not particularly worse either, just ordinary. Only the awakened, looking with the penetrating eyes of the Buddhas and the Patriarchs, constantly illuminating the entire universe, are able to testify to this fact.

Since Buddhist trainees do not do anything for the sake of themselves, how could they do anything for the sake of fame and profit? You should train for the sake of the Buddha-dharma alone. The various Buddhas do not show deep compassion for all sentient beings for either their own or others' sakes. This is the Buddhist tradition.

The awakened practice the Buddha-dharma not for themselves, let alone for fame and profit, but only for the sake of the Buddha-dharma. When they are hungry, they just eat. They don't eat in order to take a shit and don't take a shit in order to make manure. Our deluded society has it all upside down. Hardly anybody does anything for its own sake, but just in order to get results.

As Helen Tworkov put it: "This is a far cry from meditating for world peace or for the planet. Dogen Zenji asks that we renounce any sense of investment, desire, compensation, greed, or goal that we bring to meditation, to renounce our materialistic tendency to want something from it or to use it to attain our ideas of what is good or right. As a theory, this is Zen at its most bare-boned and radical and may be especially hard to swallow for well-intentioned activists."[5]

What is the obstacle? The mind creates a barrier and thinks that there must be something to go through in order to be fulfilled and liberated. It always creates another shore to cross over to, because somehow this shore is not good enough. It creates a wall and then the illusion that there is a window to pass through. There is no barrier to begin with, nor a window to go through. The other shore does not exist. If this shore is not enough, it's too bad.

Shakyamuni Buddha pointed this out very precisely in the Eight Awarenesses, his last teachings before he died. He said, "Have few desires," and then, "Know how to be satisfied with what you have." Could it be more simple and straightforward? If you are ready to accept things as they are, conflict and pain will subside. This doesn't mean you're always going to be happy. Somebody close to you may die, and of course you should grieve. It's only natural. To accept things as they are means to be one with whatever is going on. It has nothing to do with accepting or rejecting. You don't need to accept everything in the sense of liking it all, or being apathetic or complacent. The point is just to be one with whatever arises—without attachment, without rejection. Just take life as it is and start from there.

Buddhas and Patriarchs show deep compassion for all sentient beings, not for their own sake or even for the sake of others, only because they have no choice. Their very existence is the true compassion. They are not doing anything particularly to be compassionate. They have no such notion in their mind, because they have no mind. They are just being, doing what they need to do, and all sentient beings reap innumerable benefits from their actions. When people with deluded understanding try to do good and be compassionate, they only make matters worse. It is only by awakening the Bodhi-mind that compassion functions selflessly.

Master Obaku said:

> The building up of good and evil both involve attachment to form. Those who, being attached to form, do evil have to undergo various incarnations unnecessarily; while those who, being attached to form, do good, subject themselves to toil and privation equally to no purpose. In either case it is better to achieve sudden self-realization and to grasp the fundamental Dharma. This Dharma is Mind, beyond which there is no Dharma; and this Mind is the Dharma, beyond which there is no mind. Mind in itself is not mind, yet neither is it no-mind. To say that Mind is no-mind implies something existent. Let there be a silent understanding and no more. Away with all thinking and explaining. Then we may say that the way of Words has been cut off and the movements of the mind eliminated. This Mind

is the pure Buddha-source inherent in all men. All wriggling beings possessed of sentient life and all the Buddhas and Bodhisattvas are of this one substance and do not differ. Differences arise from wrong thinking only and lead to the creation of all kinds of karma.[6]

Observe how even animals and insects nurture their young, enduring various hardships in the process. The parents stand to gain nothing by their actions, even after their offspring have reached maturity. Yet, though they are only small creatures, they have deep compassion for their young. This is also the case with regard to the various Buddhas' compassion for all sentient beings. The excellent teachings of these various Buddhas, however, are not limited to compassion alone; rather, they appear in countless ways throughout the universe. This is the essence of the Buddha-dharma.

When you observe how even animals and insects take care of their young, enduring various hardships in the process, you realize that this is the Way. The deluded, however, because of their dualistic mind, think that if they take care of others, they are doing something special. They're so busy with the idea of taking care, that they may not actually do what is really needed.

Compassion does not always look like we conventionally think it should. Some animals push their young around roughly in order to help them grow strong. They stand to gain nothing for all their efforts, and yet they are ready to give everything to their offspring. These creatures show deep compassion for their young, not out of some idea of being compassionate, but only as a natural functioning of the Way. How can Buddhas be otherwise?

Their great teaching is not limited to compassion alone,

but appears in countless ways, which are impossible for ordinary people to perceive. The perception of ordinary people is limited. They are unable to see the innumerable benefits that we all are receiving continuously from these enlightened beings. Who can judge with the petty mind the extent or depth of the actions of even a single Buddha?

We are already the children of the Buddha; therefore we should follow in his footsteps. Trainees, do not practice the Buddha-dharma for your own benefit, for fame and profit, or for rewards and miraculous powers. Simply practice the Buddha-dharma for its own sake; this is the true Way.

Since we are already the children of the Buddha, we should follow the Way of the Buddha. As long as you are ignorant of this fact, then you can justify following other ways; but from the moment you awaken to the true Buddha-mind, you can no longer be so naive as to follow dualistic teachings and people with deluded understanding.

As a Zen practitioner, you should practice the Buddha-dharma for the sake of the Buddha-dharma alone, and not to gain benefit for yourself. If you are seeking to gain something from your practice, such as miraculous powers, you are far from the Way. Take heed: in the end what you gain will amount to nothing, but what you stand to lose is everything. When you practice zazen, just sit for the sake of sitting, not to gain something. When you walk in meditation, just walk; don't try to be mindful. When you eat, just eat; don't try to be spiritual. When you drive your car, just drive; don't try to kill anyone. Practice the Way for the sake of the Way only.

The forty-second Patriarch, Ryozan Osho, attended upon the Second Doan Zenji. The Patriarch asked him, "What is that beneath your kesa?" The Master did not respond. The Patriarch said, "It is most painful when one who studies Buddhism has not yet reached that stage. Now you ask me— I'll tell you." The Master said, "What is that beneath your *kesa*?" The Patriarch said, "Intimate." The Master immediately had great satori.[7]

Keizan Zenji wrote a poem about this case:

The water is deeply clear, to the very bottom;
Without being polished, it is bright by its nature.

For the teacher, it is most painful to see followers of the Way who have been practicing for a long time and who have not yet realized "it." Not knowing is most intimate. Keizan Zenji is emphasizing that your life is pure and genuine to begin with. What are you trying to polish? It is bright and clear by its very nature.

Notes

[1] Dogen Zenji, "Bendowa," in Nishiyama, *Shobogenzo*, Volume One, 149.

[2] Rinzai, 18.

[3] Jamgon Kongtrul, *The Torch of Certainty* (Boston: Shambhala, 1977), 130.

[4] Rinzai, 20–21.

[5] Helen Tworkov, *Tricycle*, winter 1993, Editor's View, 4.

[6] Huang Po, 34–35.

[7] Keizan Zenji, *Denkoroku*, unpublished translation by Koun Yamada and Robert Aitken, Case 42.

Points to Watch in Practicing the Way
Point Five

The Need to Seek a True Master

A former Patriarch once said, "If the Bodhi-mind is untrue, all one's training will come to nothing." This saying is indeed true. Furthermore, the quality of the disciple's training depends upon the truth or falsity of his master.

Master Rinzai said:

Followers of the Way, the leaver of home must study the Way. I myself was formerly interested in the Vinaya [rules and regulations] and diligently studied the Sutras and Treatises. Then I realized that they were only drugs suitable for appeasing the ills of the world, only relative theories. At one stroke I threw them away, set myself to learn the Way, started Zen training and met great teachers. Only then did my eye of the Way begin to see clearly, and I was able to understand all the old masters and to know the false from the true. Man born of woman does not naturally know this. But after long and painful practice, one morning it is realized in one's own body.

Followers of the Way, if you wish to see this Dharma clearly, do not let yourselves be deceived. Whether you turn to the outside or to the inside, whatever you encounter, kill it. If you meet the Buddha, kill the Buddha; if you meet the Patriarchs, kill the Patriarchs; if you meet Arhats, kill Arhats; if you meet your parents, kill your parents; if you meet your relatives, kill your relatives; then for the first time you will see clearly. And if you do not depend on things, there is deliverance, there is freedom![1]

If you practice with the idea that you are going to gain something, then you are heading in the wrong direction. The more you try, the further astray you will go. If you don't realize from the beginning that you are going to gain nothing from practice, and if you don't hear this over and over again and thoroughly grasp it, then you surely will gain nothing from practice.

The Buddhist trainee can be compared to a fine piece of timber, and a true master to a good carpenter. Even quality wood will not show its fine grain unless it is worked on by a good carpenter. Even a warped piece of wood will, if handled by a good carpenter, soon show the results of good craftsmanship. The truth or falsity of enlightenment depends upon whether or not one has a true master. This should be well understood.

Only under the guidance of a true master can you accomplish the Way. A fine teacher, like a gifted artist, can inspire you to reach your greatest potential. Dogen Zenji's analogy is reminiscent of Michelangelo. Just by looking at a rough block of stone he could already discern a complete sculpture. He had only to remove all the excess material to liberate this beautiful form.

The truth or falsity of one's enlightenment depends primarily upon whether one studies under a true master or not. It is easy to deceive oneself. Unless the teacher's enlightenment is genuine, the student will never accomplish the Buddha Way. There have been many who have practiced very diligently for years, but because they did not train under an enlightened Zen master they were unable to cut the root of dualistic thinking.

In our country, however, there have not been any true masters since ancient times. We can tell this by looking at their words, just as we can tell the nature of the source of a river by scooping up some of its water downstream.

How many teachers of today speak so freely as the great Master Rinzai:

> Followers of the Way, you take the words that issued from the mouths of old teachers, saying, "this is the True Way, this old sage is wonderful; I am but an ordinary fellow and dare not compare myself with such great masters." Blind fools! Your whole life you hold such views, going against the evidence of your single eye, trembling like asses on ice, your teeth clenched with fear.
>
> I am not afraid to speak out against these teachers nor of speech that is productive of Karma. Followers of the Way, only a great teacher dares to disparage the Buddhas and Patriarchs, dares to criticize everything, to

defy the Teachings of the Three Baskets, and abuse immature students, and so, whether straight or crooked, find the man within. For a dozen years I have been looking for one who is suitable, but have not been able to find as much as a mustard seed. I am afraid those Zen teachers are rather like newly wed brides, uneasy and worried about being chased out of their homes and starving to death.

Since olden times people have not believed the old masters, and only after they had been driven away did their greatness become known. He who is approved by everyone, what good is he? 'The lion's roar shatters the brain of the jackal.'[2]

Finding a true teacher has never been easy. Maybe it is even more difficult in our day and age than in olden times.

For centuries masters in this country have compiled books, taught disciples, and led both human and celestial beings. Their words, however, were still green, still unripe, for they had not yet reached the ultimate in training. They had not yet reached the sphere of enlightenment. Instead, they merely transmitted words and made others recite names and letters. Day and night they counted the treasure of others, without gaining anything for themselves.

These words show the deep compassion of Zen Master Dogen. His whole life was devoted to ensuring that the true Dharma take root in Japan. He was concerned that there were Buddhist teachers whose realization was sorely deficient and who had not reached the ultimate in training. They had not had the good fortune to be able to undergo the process of complete surrender to an authentic master. Though they compiled books and taught disciples, these self-proclaimed teachers had not yet reached enlightenment and held no true Dharma lineage. Master Dogen had contempt for these *sravakas* and *prateykabuddhas*, who through their own self-deception misled students by discouraging them from practicing that which is true and difficult. They merely transmitted eloquent words and concepts but never went to the depth of the Dharma. Instead of allowing their followers to discover their own Buddha treasure deep within, they counted the treasures of others without really becoming one with the Buddha-dharma themselves.

If the true Dharma does not take root here in the West, it is the teachers who must be held responsible, not the students. There are those who are teaching disciples and compiling books who have not yet cut the root of dualistic understanding and truly ripened in their own practice. They have not yet reached the ultimate training of the true Dharma that Dogen Zenji transmitted in Japan. Having not attained the sphere of enlightenment, they merely transmit words and concepts. Their students therefore are unable to find their way out of the mire of delusion and endless suffering. They will never be able to reveal their own Buddha treasure, but will be forced to count the treasures of others. This is truly sad.

These ancient masters must be held responsible for this state of affairs. Some of them taught that enlightenment should be sought outside the mind, others that rebirth in the Pure Land[3] was the goal. Herein lies the source of both confusion and delusion.

These ancient masters are responsible for the state of affairs today. Having not clarified the Way themselves, they taught that enlightenment could be found outside the mind, or that by praying or repeating the names of the Buddha one could be reborn in the Pure Land. This is still a great source of confusion. Of course there are some teachers today who have little understanding of the true Buddha-dharma. It is not particularly their fault, but the fault of their teachers. The fact that they have not been able to cut the root of delusion and free themselves, let alone others, is only due to the poor training they received under the guidance of their teachers.

Even if good medicine is given to someone, unless that person has also been given the proper directions for taking it, the illness may be made worse; in fact, taking medicine may do more harm than taking poison. Since ancient times there have not been any good doctors in our country who were capable of making out the correct prescription or distinguishing between medicine and poison. For this reason it has been extremely difficult to eliminate life's suffering and disease. How, then, can we expect to escape from the sufferings of old age and death?

The Buddha-dharma is the best medicine, but only if clear directions as to how to practice it are given. Without such directions the practice of zazen could even make the ailment worse. In fact, to practice zazen without the proper guidance could do more harm than taking poison. Since ancient times there have not been many good doctors in this country who were able to give the true teaching. Some unfortunately have been unable even to distinguish medicine from poison. It is for this reason that you have not been able to eliminate your suffering and free yourself from bondage. For even though you may practice zazen for years, without a true master you will still be unable to free yourself from your dualistic mind. If you cannot go beyond good and evil you cannot expect to escape from the sufferings of old age and death.

This situation is completely the fault of the masters, not of the disciples. Why? Because they guide their disciples along the branches of the tree, dispensing with its roots. Before they fully understand the Way themselves, they devote themselves solely to their own egoistic minds, luring others into the world of delusion. How regrettable it is that even these masters are unaware of their own delusion. How can their disciples be expected to know the difference between right and wrong?

The current situation is the fault of the teachers, not of present-day students, because they ignored the root of the matter and got distracted by the branches and leaves of the tree. What is the root that has been ignored? It is delusion. Dualistic thinking. Almost no one is really taking care of this matter. Wherever you turn you see people getting sidetracked by all kinds of other issues. Without cutting off dualistic and conceptual thinking completely, the ailment of the world will never be cured!

These teachers, before they have fully realized the Way, have devoted themselves solely to their own egoistic minds, luring naive students into delusion. It is sad enough that these teachers are unaware of their own delusion. How can their students be expected to know the difference between right and wrong?

Unfortunately, the true Buddha-dharma has not yet spread to this peripheral little country, and true masters have yet to be born. If you want to study the supreme Way, you have to visit mas-

ters in faraway Sung China, and reflect there on the true road that is far beyond the delusive mind. If you are unable to find a true master, it is best not to study Buddhism at all. True masters are those who have realized the true Dharma and received the seal of a genuine master. It has nothing to do with their age. For them neither learning nor knowledge is of primary importance. Possessing extraordinary power and influence, they do not rely on selfish views or cling to any obsession, for they have perfectly harmonized knowledge and practice. These are the characteristics of a true master.

Unfortunately the Buddha-dharma is not yet firmly rooted in the West. Don't be deceived! This is a very critical time for the Dharma. There are very few true masters who have yet been born in the Western world. If you really want to study the Supreme Way, you may have to travel quite far to find one.

If you are not able to find a true master, you are probably better off not to study the Buddha Way at all. Authentic masters are those who have realized the true Dharma and received the mind-seal of the Buddha. It has nothing at all to do with age, sex, or nationality. Neither learning nor knowledge is the crucial matter. These masters possess extraordinary power and influence. They do not rely on their own selfish views or cling to any obsession, for they have perfectly harmonized wisdom and practice. These are the characteristics of a true master and what you should look for when you are seeking to find a teacher.

How do you know whether you have found the right teacher? You have to follow your own intuition. Only a heart-to-heart connection makes true communion possible. What is required is faith in your teacher's realization and his ability to help you accomplish the Way.

Approaching a teacher, you walk on uncertain ground. Nobody has any idea what is going to happen. A true teacher lives in the present moment and responds to the living situation. Because it is so unpredictable it never feels safe. There are people who say that students need to feel safe with a teacher; but with a true master, there is always risk involved. How can you feel safe with someone who carries a double-edged sword, giving and taking life without blinking an eye?

Master Engo says: "When right and wrong are intermingled, even the holy ones cannot distinguish between them. When positive and negative are interwoven, even the Buddha fails to discern one from the other. The most distinguished man of transcendent experience cannot avoid showing his ability as a great master. He walks the ridge of an iceberg, he treads the edge of a sword. He is like the *kirin's* horn, like the lotus flower in the fire.[4] Meeting a man of transcendent experience, he identifies with him as his equal. Who is he?"[5]

The true master is a living koan, a walking and talking paradox, shattering all expectations and fixed ideas about the Dharma. If you keep a safe distance you may be able to hold on to such ideas, but as you get closer these ideas are destroyed. Just by being ordinary, the teacher will eventually disappoint your expectations. Simultaneously all hopes and illusions about yourself drop off. In a way the teacher is only a vehicle. The point is to cut the root of your dualistic mind and live beyond sanity and madness.

Notes

[1] Rinzai, 21.

[2] Rinzai, 16.

[3] Pure Land: the transcendent paradise from which retro-gression is no longer possible, the final stage of rebirth just prior to nirvana.

[4] The kirin is a legendary creature famous for being difficult to capture. Its horn is as rare as the unicorn's (Sekida, 260).

[5] Sekida, 258–59.

Points to Watch in Practicing the Way
Point Six

Advice for the Practice of Zen

The study of the Way through the practice of zazen is of vital importance. You should not neglect it or treat it lightly. In China there are the excellent examples of former Zen masters who cut off their arms or fingers. Long ago the Buddha Shakyamuni renounced both his home and his kingdom—another fine trace of the practice of the Way. Men of the present day, however, say that one need only practice that which is easily practiced. Their words are very mistaken and far removed from the Way. If you devote yourself to one thing exclusively and consider it to be training, even lying down will become tedious. If one thing becomes tedious, all things become tedious. You should know that those who like easy things are, as a matter of course, unworthy of the practice of the Way.

There are many examples of people who have had to go to one extreme or another to come to terms with their lives. Struck by the human condition—the reality of pain, old age, and death—and not satisfied with their understanding of these things, they started practicing zazen. Zazen is the essence of the Buddha-dharma, the direct way to liberation, but it is not an easy path. It requires a strong resolve.

If you wish to study the Buddha Way, then the practice of zazen is vitally important. You should neither neglect it nor treat it lightly. In order to negotiate the Way, single-minded wholehearted sitting cannot be dispensed with. The history of Zen has been filled with countless examples of great Zen masters who have gone through difficult training, abandoning body, mind, and home for the sake of the Way. If you do not give up attachment to body and mind, you will never accomplish the Buddha Way. Letting go of body and mind is the accomplishment of the Buddha Way. It is very easy to overlook this point and get caught up with all kinds of other matters. This is as true today in our society as it was in the time of Zen Master Dogen. The practice of zazen can easily be neglected in favor of other activities that don't bring us closer to the practice but actually lead us away from it. Profit-making can even become the primary focus. If you want to make enough money in order to practice, you may never do it. If you let go of such concerns, somehow there is always enough to practice the Way. The worst is when the importance of zazen is minimized and those who emphasize a strong sitting practice are criticized. This can only come from a lack of understanding of the Way.

The Buddha Shakyamuni left home, wife, and newborn child, giving up his position as heir to his father's kingdom, in order to become a wandering ascetic and seek the Way. The Second Patriarch of China, Eka, sliced off his arm to show Bodhidharma his determination to receive the teaching. Fifteen-year-old Kyozan Eja cut off two of his fingers when his parents refused him permission to become a monk. In whatever way we appreciate these examples, nothing short of complete relinquishment will do for attaining true peace of mind.

People today in the West, however, say that one need only practice that which is easily practiced. Students are not encouraged to practice that which is difficult and to relinquish their life, following the path of the Buddhas and Patriarchs. Teachers who inspire their students to give up home, country, comfort, and possessions and devote their whole life to zazen might even be seen as irresponsible or mad. In our society it seems absurd to devote one's whole life to doing absolutely nothing.

If you devote yourself exclusively even to a practice which is easy and consider this to be training, whatever you are doing will become tiresome and lose its life. So why not devote your life to single-minded zazen and the Way of the Buddhas and the Patriarchs?

Those who like to take it easy and do not really put themselves completely into zazen and practice shall never realize the Way of the Buddhas. In the *Shobogenzo Zuimonki* Dogen Zenji said, "Without exception everyone is a vessel of the Buddha-dharma. Never think that you are not a vessel. If you practice according to the teaching, you will gain realization without fail. Since you have a mind, you are able to distinguish false from true. You have hands and feet, therefore you lack nothing to practice bowing or walking. Consequently, in practicing the Buddha-dharma do not be concerned with whether you are capable or not. Living beings in the human world are all vessels of the Buddha-dharma."[1]

If you practice in accord with the teaching, just doing zazen with your whole heart, not seeking gain or reward, you will inevitably attain realization. You are responsible for distinguishing true from false teaching. If you cannot, you have no one to blame but yourself. Do not be concerned with whether or not you have the capacity to do real practice. Only have faith in the Way. You are already a vessel for the Dharma. Never doubt this fact. Do not study with teachers who have deluded understanding or dualistic views. They will only mislead you into practicing that which is easy and teach you to be content with a "normal" life. They will discourage you from total relinquishment. The Buddha Shakyamuni gave everything up in order to pursue the Way. All the great Patriarchs did likewise.

Our great teacher, Shakyamuni, was unable to gain the teaching that prevails in the present world until after he had undergone severe training for countless ages in the past. Considering how dedicated the founder of Buddhism was, can his descendants be any less so? Those who seek the Way should not look for easy training. Should you do so, you will never be able to reach the true world of enlightenment or find the treasure house. Even the most gifted of the former Patriarchs have said that the Way is difficult to practice. You should realize how deep and immense Buddhism is. If the Way were, originally, so easy to practice and understand, these former gifted Patriarchs would not have stressed its difficulty. By comparison with the former Patriarchs, people of today do not amount to even as much as a single hair in a herd of nine cows! That is to say, even if these moderns, lacking as they do both ability and knowledge, exert themselves to the utmost, their imagined difficult practice would still be incomparable to that of the former Patriarchs.

After many lives of hard training, the Buddha was born as Shakyamuni; but even then he practiced arduous yoga and prolonged fasting until he found that extremes of hardship did not bring him any more fulfillment than the other extreme, the life of luxury he had known as a prince in his father's palace. His last resort was zazen. He practiced zazen for six years before he sat down under a tree and vowed to stay there until realization would dawn upon him. On the morning of the eighth day of December, as he glanced up and saw the planet Venus fading from the sky, he had his great enlightenment. If even the Buddha had to apply himself like that, how can we ever hope to accomplish the way without giving ourself completely?

Strong sitting allows us to get to the root of reality. The Dharma is so profound that only deep *samadhi* can reach it. If we hold back we'll just stay on a superficial level, fiddling around with the leaves and branches. We must go to the very root of our dualistic consciousness and cut it off completely.

The key to this is zazen. Throughout the ages people have tried just about everything, but how many of them have really attained the Way? Whatever we do or believe in, without the practice of zazen the treasure house remains closed.

What might Dogen Zenji have said about our practice of the Dharma today in the West? All the great Patriarchs have confirmed that the Way is difficult to practice. To gain a shallow understanding of Zen is not difficult, but to realize the depth and breadth of the Buddha Way is not so easy. In our Western society it is tempting to become sidetracked with earning a living, maintaining a household, and climbing the social ladder. Not that any of these things are bad; only we shouldn't confuse this with practicing the Way of the Buddhas and Patriarchs.

That is to say, even if these moderns, lacking as they do both ability and knowledge, exert themselves to the utmost, their imagined difficult practice would still be incomparable to that of the former great Patriarchs.

What is the easily practiced and easily understood teaching of which present-day man is so fond? It is neither a secular teaching nor a Buddhist one. It is even inferior to the practice of demons and evil spirits, as well as to that of non-Buddhist religions and sravakas and pratyekabuddhas. It may be said to be the great delusion of ordinary men and women. Although they imagine that they have escaped from the delusive world, they have, on the contrary, merely subjected themselves to endless transmigration.

What are these practices of which present-day man is so fond? Dogen Zenji means here all the practices which are based on dualistic understanding, dividing body and mind, life and death, good and evil, light and dark, right and wrong, enlightened and deluded. The equivalent today of the *sravakas* and *prateykabuddhas* would be those who have not undergone the complete training required under an authentic master and start teaching the Dharma without going through the difficult process of surrendering to the Way.

What is the great delusion of ordinary men and women? Trying to escape from suffering by turning to teachings that will never give true satisfaction. From a Dharma perspective, any teaching that does not cut the root of delusion, however helpful for other purposes, offers only partial truth. It may give people the illusion that they have escaped from the delusive world, but they have merely subjected themselves to endless transmigration. Transmigration refers to repeated rebirth into lifetime after lifetime of suffering without liberation. While holding on to dualistic views of self and other, we have no opportunity to break out of this endless cycle.

Breaking one's bones and crushing the marrow to gain Buddhism are thought to be difficult practices. It is still more difficult, however, to control the mind, let alone undergo prolonged austerities and pure training, while controlling one's physical actions is most difficult of all.

There are no shortcuts. To study and forget the self will always be difficult. That is why long hours of training are necessary. Most people need an environment that supports their sitting and is conducive to dropping their habitual patterns. At home it is too easy to escape. How many can bring themselves to sit as much as students do in a training center? Moreover, by fitting yourself into a program you learn to be flexible and to put your own ideas aside. While students work closely together, rubbing against one another like pebbles in a mountain stream, their rough edges are steadily worn down and they become more polished. Without such training you have no opportunity to refine your practice and harmonize mind and body. What better way is there to maintain the precepts than sitting in zazen? Relinquishing one's personal life, living and practicing like this, is the Supreme Way.

If the crushing of one's bones were of value, the many who endured this training in the past should have realized enlightenment; but in fact, only a few did. If the practice of austerities were of value, the many who have done so since ancient times also should have become enlightened; but here, too, only a few did. This all stems from the great difficulty of controlling the mind. In Buddhism neither a brilliant mind nor scholastic understanding is of primary importance. The same holds true for intellect, volition, consciousness, memory, imagination, and contemplation. None of these are of any use, for the Way may be entered only through the harmonization of body and mind.

Going through hardship gives one no guarantee. There are people who undergo tremendous suffering, but in the end become no wiser for it. Everything depends on how you respond to whatever is happening in your life. To learn to respond with compassion, you have to become one with your own mind and cease from relying on standard formulas. Only when you turn your own light inward, illuminating the self, body and mind will drop off naturally and original self will manifest.

In practicing the Buddha-dharma, neither a brilliant mind nor scholastic understanding is of primary importance. The same holds true for a keen intellect, volition, consciousness, and contemplation. None of these are of any use, for the Way may be entered only through the harmonization of body and mind. Harmonization of body and mind comes about in zazen, by transcending all dichotomies: movement and non-movement, self and other, sane and mad, good and evil.

Cutting off dualistic thinking does not mean that you should do bad things and neglect doing good. No one can ignore the law of causation. It means you no longer think in terms of absolutes. You don't hold a Buddha view nor a Dharma view, much less a view of what is right or wrong. You are free to act according to the needs of the present situation out of *prajna* wisdom and compassion, rather than coming from deluded understanding.

The Buddha Shakyamuni said, "Turning the sound-perceiving stream of the mind inward, forsake knowing and being known." This is what harmonizing body and mind means. The two qualities of movement and nonmovement have not appeared at all; this is true harmony.

The Buddha had to forsake both knowing and not knowing. As Master Nansen said to Joshu, "Knowing is not it, not knowing is also not it; knowing is delusion, not knowing mere blankness."[2] Zazen is harmonizing body and mind. There is no separation, but in order to realize that, you need to cut the root of dualistic thinking.

Harmonizing body and mind means dropping off all attachments to body and mind and cutting through the dualistic notion of body and mind being two. How can you realize that body and mind are one as long as you are completely attached to body and mind? "Mind" includes all your thoughts, concepts, ideas, and dualistic beliefs.

When the two qualities of movement and nonmovement, action and stillness, do not appear at all, this is true harmony of body and mind. It goes beyond all dualities such as you and me, movement and stillness, life and death, enlightened or deluded.

If it were possible to enter the Way on the basis of having a brilliant mind and wide knowledge, high-ranking Jinshu should certainly have been able to do so. If common birth were an obstacle to entering the Way, how did Eno become one of the Chinese Patriarchs? These examples clearly show that the process of transmitting the Way does not depend on either a brilliant mind or wide knowledge. In seeking the true Dharma, reflect on yourselves and train diligently.

Again Dogen Zenji is emphasizing that just having a brilliant mind and a great deal of knowledge is not enough to accomplish the Way. Master Eno was born in the year 638 to a poor family, but with a rich spiritual endowment. Hearing someone chanting the Diamond Sutra inspired him to seek a true teacher at an early age. He traveled all the way from the south to the north of China where the Fifth Patriarch, Master Gunin, lived on Mount Obai. Eno arrived at the monastery when he was twenty-four, a shabby, illiterate youth. Master Gunin recognized his spiritual clarity at their first encounter and allowed Eno to stay in the monastery as a rice-cleaner. Eno was not permitted to sit with the monks because of his poor background.

One day Master Gunin announced to his more than seven hundred disciples, "Each one of you, make a poem to express your own realization and show whether you are worthy to be my Dharma successor." In response, Jinshu, the most senior and respected monk in the monastery, wrote the following poem on the monastery wall:

> The body is the tree of bodhi,
> The mind is like the stand of a bright mirror.
> Moment by moment wipe the mirror carefully,
> Never let dust collect on it.

Eno admired Jinshu's verse, but didn't feel it penetrated to the core; it still showed a trace of dualistic thinking and did not present the absolute reality. He made a poem to express his own understanding and asked someone to write it on the wall also:

> Bodhi is not originally a tree,
> Nor has the bright mirror a stand.
> Originally there is nothing,
> So where can any dust collect?

Master Gunin recognized Eno's superior realization and gave him the the robe and the bowl, the symbols of Dharma transmission. This had to be done secretly, because the monks would not accept an illiterate layman as the Sixth Patriarch. Master Gunin even advised Eno to hide himself until the right opportunity arose for him to come forward.[3]

The Buddha Way does not depend on either a brilliant mind nor wide knowledge. This example shows clearly that the process of transmitting the Dharma goes far beyond either of these. Just devote yourself completely to real training and seeking the true Dharma. Don't get caught up as so many do in intellectual study and conceptual understanding. The Way does not fit into any concept and can never be grasped by the intellect, so don't try to understand the Dharma with your conceptual mind. When you listen to the teaching of a master, just let it pass through you like a cool breeze. Perhaps it triggers something deep inside you, perhaps it doesn't; but either way, don't try to figure it out or cling to it. Only reflect on yourself and practice zazen diligently, cutting off the root of dualistic thinking, if you wish to be liberated completely.

Neither youth nor age is an obstacle to entering the Way. Joshu was more than sixty years old when he first began to practice, yet he became an outstanding Patriarch. Tei's daughter, on the other hand, was only thirteen years old, but she had already attained a deep understanding of the Way, so much so that she became one of the finest trainees in her monastery.

Age has nothing to do with it. A child can enter the Way, as can someone close to death. Neither age, sex, intelligence, nor physical ability has anything to do with it. The Way is only accomplished by training and casting away body and mind under the guidance of a true teacher.

Obviously it is never too late to begin practicing. Dogen Zenji presents here a different account of Joshu's life, possibly just to make this point. It is generally believed that Joshu became a monk at a very young age, attained enlightenment at eighteen, then studied under Master Nansen for forty more years. Nansen died in 834 when Joshu was sixty. Not completely satisfied, he travelled around meeting various masters for more then twenty years. When he left Nansen's monastery he told himself, "Even a seven-year-old child, if he is greater than I am, I'll ask him to teach me. Even a hundred-year-old man, if I am greater than he is, I'll teach him."[4] Perhaps Dogen Zenji refers to this period of Joshu's development as real practice. In any case, only at the age of eighty did he settle down and become the abbot of the Kannonin in Joshu. He is revered as one of the greatest Patriarchs in the history of Zen.

By referring to Tei's daughter, Dogen Zenji is making the point that attaining deep realization into the meaning of life and death does not depend on either age or gender. In our contemporary Western world, women have the same opportunity as men do. There is the potential now in the West for some really great women Dharma successors to appear.

The majesty of Buddhism appears according to whether or not the effort is made, and differs according to whether or not training with a teacher is involved.

If we want the majesty of Buddhism to take root in our Western culture, we cannot neglect what Master Dogen is saying here: it will appear only according to whether or not the effort is made, and differs according to whether or not training with a genuine teacher is involved. If we neglect either of these two aspects, the true Buddha-dharma will not take root in the Western world.

Those who have long devoted themselves to the study of the sutras, as well as those who are well versed in secular learning, should visit a Zen monastery. There are many examples of those who have done so. Nangaku Eshi was a man of many talents, yet he trained under Bodhidharma. Yoka Genkaku was the finest of men; still he trained under Daikan Eno. The clarification of the Dharma and the realization of the Way are dependent upon the power gained from training under Zen masters.

Nangaku Eshi and Genkaku were both prominent representatives of the Chinese Tendai school. Gengaku was so gifted that he grasped Master Eno's Dharma during their first encounter. However accomplished these two masters were already, they still sought instruction from a Zen teacher who they felt had greater understanding. Since ancient times, those who wished to truly accomplish the Way have given up the study of religious and secular texts and practiced zazen under a true teacher.

Maezumi Roshi is fortunate to have trained under more than three eminent teachers. Once he said that his only regret was that they have all passed away. When Nishiwaki Roshi, successor to Harada Roshi, was in the United States in 1981, Maezumi Roshi went to *dokusan* with him at every opportunity. After going through koan study in two different lineages, Roshi was still eager to clarify his understanding further with another teacher.

Soen Roshi also expressed this kind of aspiration. After he was made abbot of Ryotaku-ji he decided to start koan study with Yasutani Roshi, a master from a different tradition. I have great respect for him. It is said that he would always take off the colored robe of a Dharma holder and put on the black *kesa* of a simple monk whenever he would go to see his teacher. The clarification of the Dharma and the realization of the Way are dependent upon the power gained from training under Zen masters.

> *When visiting a Zen master to seek instruction, listen to his teaching without trying to make it conform to your own self-centered viewpoint; otherwise you will be unable to understand what he is saying. Purifying your own body and mind, eyes and ears, simply listen to his teaching, expelling any other thought. Unify your body and mind and receive the master's teaching as if water were being poured from one vessel into another. If you do so, then for the first time you will be able to understand his teaching.*

When receiving instruction from a true Zen teacher, the best thing to do is to drop all preconceived ideas and empty the mind; just listen to the teaching without trying to make it conform to your own views. If you don't do this, you will not be able to grasp the true teaching. It is difficult to know how to really listen. We are inclined to hear the teaching the way we want to hear it and twist it around to fit our own ideas.

A master transmits the Buddha-dharma, and the student is a vessel with the potential to receive it; but first the proper conditions have to be present for this transfer to be possible. The student needs to put himself in the lower position in relation to the teacher. However big or beautiful the student's vessel is, if it sits right next to, above, or far away from the teacher, nothing can be poured into it. Furthermore, the container needs to be empty and clean in order to receive the teaching purely. If the student is full of preconceived notions, the essence of the teaching will be diluted.

Finally, after receiving the Dharma properly, the bottom of the bucket has to be dropped out. What good is it to keep the teaching for oneself? It will only become stagnant. A real vessel of the Dharma is more like a tube, completely open at both ends. Only in this way can the Dharma flow freely through us.

At present, there are some foolish people who either devote themselves to memorizing the words and phrases of the sutras or attach themselves to that which they have heard before. Having done so, they try to equate these with the teachings of a living master. Their minds are filled with their personal views and ancient sayings. They will never be able to become one with their teacher's words. Still others, attaching primary importance to their own self-centered thinking, open the sutras and memorize a word or two, imagining this to be the Buddha-dharma. Later when they are taught the Dharma by an enlightened Zen master, they regard his teaching as true if it corresponds with their own views; otherwise they regard it as false. Not knowing how to give up this mistaken way of thinking, they are unable to return to the true Way. They are to be pitied, for they will remain deluded for countless kalpas. How regrettable!

At present, there are those who are attached to the words and phrases of ancient masters. They then try to compare the teachings they have learned with the teachings of the living master. Their minds are filled with personal views and ancient sayings. They will never be able to become one with their master. There are others who attach primary importance to their own deluded and self-centered thinking, memorizing words from texts, imagining this to be the true Buddha-dharma. When they finally come into contact with the true Dharma taught by an awakened Zen master, they only regard his teaching as true if it corresponds to their own views; oth-

79

erwise they regard it as false. They are unable to return to the true Way, not knowing how to give up their mistaken way of thinking. They will remain deluded for lifetimes, and are to be pitied. This is truly regrettable.

When you read something that supports your own point of view, it is tempting to use it as a standard. Your opinions will only grow stronger if they are backed up by someone with authority, and soon you may try to make everything fit into your criteria of good and bad. When you work closely with a teacher, you have to empty your mind of all such ideas, both your own notions and those you have accumulated from others.

If you are not willing to let go of your convictions, you'll fail to receive the teaching. Even if you cling to your own teacher's words you'll miss it, because the next day he or she may say something completely different. The Sixth Patriarch once said that if a student says "up" the teacher says "down"; if a student says "black," the teacher says "white." Master Rinzai used to talk a lot about dropping the ceaselessly seeking mind, but when one of his monks finally announced that he had dropped it, Rinzai immediately hit him and shouted, "Go and search as hard as you can!"

The practice is not to settle any place; if you stay anywhere too long, you become attached. It could also be said that you really should settle down. Both sides are true; and yet if you cling to either one, you definitely get stuck. It is the teacher's job to keep the student flexible and unstuck all the time, even from so-called wisdom.

Any teaching becomes false teaching when you get attached to it. You have to learn to move back and forth from one perspective to another without any hindrance. Think of a scale: if the pointer cannot move, no matter where it points the scale is absolutely useless. Even enlightenment has no value if you insist on remaining there. True teaching does not leave you any place on which to stand, so you learn to settle on nothing, to be completely groundless. Then you don't have anything to depend on—no fixed notion of good or evil, right or wrong; no wisdom, no enlightenment. This is true wisdom, true enlightenment. This is to go beyond sanity and madness.

There are people who attach too much importance to their own egoistic thinking. They read books, memorizing words and phrases, imagining this to be the Buddha-dharma. Then they may set themselves up as authorities on Zen. They know a great deal from their studies and quote the sutras and sayings of great Zen masters, but they lack any true wisdom or understanding based upon their own experience. They lead others down false paths and condemn true masters.

It is always easier to read a book and stick to your own interpretations than to confront a living teacher. Books can give you the comfortable feeling that you know something. They don't show you where you are stuck. They usually don't even contradict your opinions, because it is possible to read only that which you are ready to accept and ignore the rest.

There are students who, when studying with a teacher, regard his or her teaching and behavior as correct only if it corresponds to their own views; if they are disappointed or disillusioned they regard it as false teaching and self-right-eously blame the teacher for their disappointment. Because they don't really want to give up their mistaken way of think-ing, they often stop training and miss the opportunity to accomplish the Way. They look for people who will agree with them in order to find support for their deluded ideas, wasting their lives searching for a teacher who will live up to their expectations. If they should find this perfect master, they may feel good for awhile but, never having relinquished their strongly held beliefs, they are likely to remain deluded and dissatisfied for countless kalpas. This is indeed regrettable!

Buddhist trainees should realize that the Buddha-dharma is beyond either thought, discrimination, and imagination, or insight, perception, and intellectual understanding. Were it not so, why is it that, having been endowed with these various faculties since birth, you have still not realized the Way?

It makes no sense to hold on to any view of the Buddha-dharma. It is beyond the grasp of our senses, including intellectual understanding. All perception is based on a separation between the perceiver and that which is perceived. The Buddha-dharma cannot be divided into subject and object and therefore can never be known through discrimination. Who is there to know and what is there to be known?

The Buddha-dharma is far beyond your thinking, discrimination, imagination, insight, perception, and intellectual understanding. If you don't grasp this, then there is little chance to accomplish the Way. When you study with a true teacher, put these faculties aside, wholeheartedly devoting yourself to zazen and listening to your teacher.

If the Way could be realized by using mental capacities, many more people would be enlightened by now; but even the brightest mind with the highest IQ can't come close to realization by relying on the intellect. It is only by going beyond the discriminating mind that you can really accomplish the Way.

*Thought, discrimination, and so forth should be avoided
in the practice of the Way. This will become clear if, using thought
and so on, you examine yourself carefully. The gateway to the
Truth is known only to enlightened Zen masters, not to their
learned counterparts.*

If thinking is not going to help you one iota to realize
the Way, why continue to rely on it? Thinking just keeps you
going around in circles. How long do you want to play that
game? Only when you give up trying to understand do you
gain the power to move mountains. No one caught up in
dualistic thinking can accomplish such a thing. When you
really drop off body and mind, you can turn the earth and
revolve the heavens; you can swallow all the water of the
Pacific in one gulp.

When you reflect on yourself during zazen, what do you
see? Only your own opinions and attachments, your small
and petty mind, always worrying about me and mine. To go
beyond such concerns you must drop the self. The gateway to
the Truth is known only to enlightened masters, not to their
learned counterparts.

Notes

1 Okamura, *Dogen Zen*, 26–27.
2 *Mumonkan*, Case 19, in Shibayama,140.
3 *Mumonkan*, Case 23, in Shibayama, 169.
4 *Mumonkan*, Case 1, in Shibayama, 21.

Points to Watch in Practicing the Way
Point Seven
_·_·—·—·—·—·◈·—·—·—·—·_·_

The Need for Zen Training
in Buddhist Practice and Enlightenment

Buddhism is superior to any other teaching. It is for this rea-
son that many people pursue it. During the Tathagata's lifetime,
there was only one teaching and only one teacher. The Great Master
alone led all beings with his supreme Wisdom. Since the Venerable
Mahakasyapa transmitted the Eye Storehouse of the true Dharma,
twenty-eight generations in India, six generations in China, and the
various patriarchs of the five Zen schools have transmitted it with-
out interruption. Since the P'u-t'ung era [520–526] in the Chinese
state of Liang all truly superior individuals—from monks to royal
retainers—have taken refuge in Zen Buddhism.

All teaching is limited to some degree or another. The
Buddha Way transcends teaching and therefore is the
supreme teaching. It includes everything and excludes nothing; it has no outside, no boundaries. No other teaching is so
vast and complete. For this reason many people from different
religious backgrounds practice the Buddha Way.

During the lifetime of the Buddha, his teaching was the only one that went to the heart of the problem of life and death by transcending duality. It is for this reason that his supreme Wisdom led beings to complete emancipation. In this day and age we have a great variety of teachings available, but whether or not this multitude of options is really a blessing remains to be seen.

Shakyamuni Buddha transmitted the true Dharma to the Venerable Mahakasyapa alone, who subsequently transmitted this Dharma to twenty-eight successive Patriarchs in India, six generations in China, and to the various Patriarchs of the five Zen schools without interruption. The direct transmission from teacher to student is of vital importance and rarely encountered.

Dogen Zenji had to make the long arduous journey to China to find a true master. Buddhist teaching had already reached China five hundred years before the arrival of Bodhidharma, but it consisted primarily of devotional disciplines and scholarly interpretation of the sutras. Bodhidharma was the first one to transmit the true Dharma, the practice of zazen. The impact of his presence was enormous. Not only monks but even emperors and their ministers turned to Zen. The daughter of Emperor Wu became one of Bodhidharma's four enlightened students.

Truly, excellence should be loved because of its excellence. One should not love dragons as Sekko did. In the various countries east of China the casting net of scholastic Buddhism has been spread over the seas and mountains. Even though spread over the mountains, however, it does not contain the heart of the clouds; even though spread over the seas, it lacks the heart of the waves.

The foolish are fond of this kind of Buddhism. They are delighted by it like those who take the eye of a fish to be a pearl, or those who treasure a stone from Mount Yen in the belief that it is a precious jewel. Many such people fall into the pit of demons, thereby losing their true Self.

Since zazen transcends all conditions, it is the Supreme Way. The love for zazen is only natural and deepens with continuous practice. What else could be more fulfilling? The most profound and subtle expression of life is manifested in the true posture of zazen. This is known as joyous, self-fulfilling *samadhi* (*jijuyu-zanmai*). Body and mind drop off spontaneously. If you love zazen and continue to sit with your whole heart, then eventually it will happen.

Sekko was so fond of dragons that he put statues and paintings of dragons all over his room. One day a real dragon heard of Sekko's passion and decided to pay him a visit. When Sekko saw the creature in the flesh, he was so terrified that he passed out. Concepts about Zen are like painted dragons. You can praise the virtue of practice, but to appreciate the real thing you must sit. Studying and speaking about the Way is easy but practice is difficult. Resistance to sitting arises from all the things that are difficult to face—fear, anger, boredom, jealousy, and so on—which inevitably come up in zazen.

Dogen Zenji lived in a time of great transition. The true Dharma had still to be introduced to Japan. We too are in a pioneer stage and the practice here is still fragile. Zen is popular now in the West—especially among intellectuals, artists, and psychotherapists—but true training under an authentic master is still as difficult to find today as it was in the time of Dogen Zenji. In order to make Zen accessible to Westerners,

Zen teaching has been watered down and conceptualized in some places. This has resulted in a lack of emphasis on realization, which could prevent the true Dharma from taking root in the West.

The point is to transcend intellectual understanding and doctrinal debate and clarify the heart of the clouds and the heart of the waves. What is the heart of Zen? The matter of life and death is of supreme importance and cannot be neglected.

Only the foolish are fond of a conceptual and intellectual approach to Zen. They are delighted by it like those who take the eye of a fish to be a pearl, or those who treasure a stone from Mount Yen in the belief that it is a precious jewel. Words and concepts are like colored pebbles. They may be fun to play with, but should not be confused with the precious jewel of zazen.

Having only an intellectual or conceptual understanding of Zen is dangerous, because it reinforces one's dualistic notions about good and evil, right and wrong, life and death, self and other. It limits one's perspective on life, especially when these notions are turned into codes of conduct. If Zen is allowed to move in this direction, it could easily become just as sterile as the religions so many have turned away from—religions of dogmas, rules and regulations, without any life or spirit.

The situation in remote countries like this one is truly regrettable; for here, where the winds of false teachings blow freely, it is difficult to spread the true Dharma. China, however, has already taken refuge in the true Buddha-dharma.

Dogen Zenji was looking at the situation in his native

country with a very critical eye. This is exactly what needs to be done in the West right now. Who would really be satisfied with the kind of Zen that is acceptable to the average American spiritual consumer—a bland sort of Zen, lacking in true spirit, moralistic in outlook, and based upon a dualistic conceptual understanding?

If you want to take refuge in the true Buddha-dharma, you need to have real faith in it, and mistrust easy answers and simple formulas; they will not take care of the great matter of life and death. Definitely the practice will change as it integrates into Western culture, but the spirit of the true Dharma could be lost if it is too hastily blended it into a society whose main characteristic is greed: the pursuit of fame and profit.

Why is it, then, that it has not yet spread to either our country or Korea? Although in Korea at least the name of the true Dharma can be heard, in our country even this is impossible. This is because the many teachers who went to study the Buddha-dharma in China in the past clung to the net of scholastic Buddhism. Although they transmitted various Buddhist texts, they seem to have forgotten the spirit of Buddhism. Of what value was this? In the end it came to nothing. This is all because they did not know the essence of studying the Way. How regrettable it is that they worked so hard their whole life to no purpose.

Fortunately today here in the West, unlike in Dogen Zenji's time, it is not completely impossible to practice the true Dharma under an authentic master, but it is a rare opportunity. The problem is that many who are teaching have not yet cut the root of dualistic thinking and cling to an intellectual and conceptual understanding of Buddhism. Although there is a lot of Dharma available now, genuine practice is difficult to find. Without genuine practice, the right transmission of true Dharma is not possible, so what then is the value of busying oneself with so many activities in the name of the Dharma? When all kinds of diversions—counseling, psychotherapy, businesses, creating standards of conduct, grievance committees, workshops, entertaining the rich and famous, political movements, ecology, vegetarianism, and conferences—take priority, the necessity of true practice is neglected. What gets lost is the importance of realization, genuine compassion, and the true transmission: Bodhi-mind. As Zen Master Dogen said, it is all because people do not know the essence of studying the Way.

Buddhist philosophy is so profound that one can easily get attached to words and letters; but if you don't make it your own direct experience, the whole point is lost. The teachings are the body and zazen is the heart. What is a body without a heart? Those who transmit only a dualistic and conceptual understanding of Zen miss the point completely. They get caught up in concepts of right and wrong and good and bad that have nothing to do with the true spirit of Zen.

Those who devote themselves to the study of Buddhism, but who never meet a true master and undergo real Zen training, never have a chance to receive the true teaching. Their practice has been futile. Their strenuous efforts make their failure all the more tragic. None of them manage to transmit the essence of the Buddha-dharma.

When you first enter the gateway of the Buddha-dharma and begin to study the Way, simply listen to the teaching of a Zen master and train accordingly. At that time you should know the fol-

lowing: the Dharma turns self, and self turns the Dharma. When self turns the Dharma, self is strong and the Dharma is weak. In the reverse case, the Dharma is strong and self is weak. Although Buddhism has had these two aspects since long ago, they have only been known by those who have received the true transmission. Without a true master, it is impossible to hear even the names of these two aspects.

It is by no means easy to listen to the teaching of a Zen master with an open and empty mind. Instead people come with all their preconceived notions and judge the teachings dualistically. The foolish are attached to delusive ways of thought. Here the self turns the Dharma, twisting the truth to fit preconceived notions of how things should be. This forces one into a self-righteous position and creates a rigid picture of what the teaching and compassion ought to look like. There is no incentive to give up one's attachments; this is why the mind becomes fixated. The awakened allow themselves to be guided by the Dharma, putting all of their faith and trust in it. The Dharma is then manifested as the self.

Master Engo says: "The spirit which moves like lightning you fail to follow. When the bolt descends from the blue, you have no time to cover your ears. The scarlet banner flutters over the master's head; the two-edged sword is being brandished behind the student's neck. Unless your eyes are sharp and your hands move quickly, how can you cope with the situation? One will lower his head and ponder, following the delusive ways of thought. Don't you know that countless skulls are haunted by ghosts? I want to ask you, without falling into the delusive way of thinking and without halting irresolutely, how can you respond to the teacher's words?"[1]

Unless one knows the essence of studying the Way, it is impossible to practice it; for how, otherwise, could one determine what is right and what is wrong? Those who now study the Way through the practice of zazen naturally transmit this essence. This is why there have been no mistakes made in the transmission, something that cannot be said of the other Buddhist sects. Those who seek the Buddha-dharma cannot realize the true Way without the practice of zazen.

Only those who have received the true transmission from an authentic master and have realized the essence can really know what is true or false. Unless one knows the essence of studying the Way, it is impossible to practice it; for how, otherwise, could one determine what is right and what is wrong? What is appropriate always depends on the situation and cannot be standardized, because everything is unfixed. There is no absolute right or wrong. Each situation is different, depending on person, time, and place. Who but the individual directly involved could know the circumstances?

A true master is one who has gone to the depths of practice and is intimate with the self. Realizing how bad he is, how can he pass judgment on others?

Those who study the Way naturally transmit the true Dharma through *jijuyu samadhi*. This self-fulfilling *samadhi* is the pure and incorruptible standard of the true transmission and remains the same for all Buddhas throughout space and time. This is why there have been no mistakes made when the transmission has been authentic. Those who seek the Buddha-dharma cannot realize the true Way without the practice of zazen. Dogen Zenji studied the methods of the various schools extensively and came to the realization that zazen is the only way to accomplish the Buddha-dharma. There are many practices in Buddhism, but only through the practice of zazen, dropping off body and mind, can the true transmission occur.

Dogen Zenji's brilliance is rare. He could see right through the shortcomings of any teaching. He was quite a critical person; or it could be said that he adhered to a very high standard and wanted to transmit nothing less than the gem of pure practice. He is not being judgmental; he is just stating plain fact. When you call a grey-haired person's hair grey, it is not a judgment, just a fact. If you say, "I don't like your grey hair," then it becomes a judgment. Criticism can be damaging if it is used to defend one's ego, but very valuable if it arises out of compassion. We should be extremely grateful for Dogen Zenji's unsurpassed clarity.

Those who seek the Buddha-dharma should not neglect to practice zazen. One of the problems both in the United States and Europe is the lack of strong emphasis on zazen. Other things begin to take precedence. Will the true Dharma really take root in our Western civilization? It is not so certain. The transmission of the true Buddha-dharma could easily be lost.

Notes

[1] *Hekiganroku*, Master Engo's Introduction to Case 37, in Sekida, 246–47.

Points to Watch in Practicing the Way
Point Eight

--·--·--·--·--◆--·--·--·--·--

The Conduct of Zen Monks

This chapter is about the attitude or aspiration that is required in order to practice the Way. In some of his writings Dogen Zenji points out very specific rules of behavior, but here no reference is made to any of that. The conduct he advocates here is more focused on the transmission of the Buddha-dharma than on rules and regulations.

Since the time of the Buddha, the twenty-eight Patriarchs in India and the six in China have directly transmitted the Dharma, adding not even so much as a thread or hair, nor allowing even a particle of dust to penetrate it. With the transmission of the Buddha's kesa to the Sixth Patriarch, Eno, the Buddha-dharma spread throughout the world. At present the Tathagata's treasury of the true Dharma is flourishing in China. It is impossible to realize what the Dharma is by groping or searching for it. Those who have seen the Way forget their knowledge of it, transcending relative consciousness.

The first and most important principle of right conduct for Dogen Zenji is the correct transmission of *Shobo*, the true Dharma, without any deviation. To transmit this Dharma is the right conduct of Zen monks.

> Every Buddha and each Tathagata has the wonderful ability to attain supreme and perfect enlightenment; they transmit that enlightenment from one to another without alteration. This ability transcends and is not bound by any human devices—it is *jijuyu samadhi*, the proper method and standard of the transmission from Buddha to Buddha.
>
> To achieve this *samadhi* you must enter the true gate of zazen—the best method of manifesting enlightenment. It is present in everyone, but unless there is practice it cannot be manifested, and unless there is realization it cannot be perceived. One or many, horizontal or vertical, cannot limit or describe it. Speak it and it has already filled your mouth; let it go and it fills your hands. Buddhas exist within *jijuyu samadhi* without attachment; sentient beings also exist therein, but do not realize how their consciousness and perceptions function. Through this *samadhi* we can find true reality and achieve perfect harmony—just abandon discrimination.[1]

This precious teaching has survived through the ages, and Dogen Zenji is highly concerned about passing it on to future generations. Whether you realize it or not, it is in our hands now, and if we don't share his concern, who will? Dogen Zenji is long gone; it is really up to you and me to transmit the Buddha-dharma, to make sure that not even so much as a thread or hair is added, or even a particle of dust is allowed to penetrate it. Can we take on this enormous responsibility? Can we really transmit the true Dharma without deviation and without getting sidetracked?

The greatest desire of a true master is to transmit the Dharma, to empower others to realize Buddhahood. The problem is finding students who are ready to receive it. Some may think that they are ready, but the Dharma requires total relinquishment. In order to receive the teaching without distortion, you first have to empty yourself completely and let go of all preconceived notions. That is not an easy task, because most of these notions have been gradually consolidated over the years into concepts that seem so valid and right that hardly anyone ever thinks to question them. Nobody dares. Isn't it important to have some clearcut standards by which to distinguish right from wrong? Maybe so; but who is the judge and what faculty makes these distinctions?

Dogen Zenji talks about the discriminating mind. It is exactly this mind you must drop in order to realize the Truth. You have to be ready to go beyond sanity and madness, good and evil, to cut off the root of dualistic thinking altogether. In working directly with a true master, heart to heart, you have the best possible chance to do so.

This is the essence of right conduct. It has nothing to do with our conventional understanding of correct behavior based on a fixed idea of right and wrong. Usually the precepts are interpreted and understood only from a literal perspective, as shoulds and should-nots, do's and don'ts. The precepts are absolutely essential for practicing the Buddha Way, but it is equally important not to get stuck in a too literal interpretation of them and lose the Mahayana spirit.

Furthermore, if we think that we are maintaining a pre-

97

cept on a Hinayana level—for example, "I don't tell lies"—at the very moment we raise the notion of "self" we are already breaking the precept from a Buddhayana, or One Buddha-mind, perspective. All of us are responsible for our actions and reactions. There is no one else to blame for situations we find ourselves in, because we are creating our own karma continuously. This karma is constantly changing, and it is up to each individual to be aware of the appropriateness of what to say and do. Taking on this full responsibility must come out of wisdom and compassion.

Everyone is endowed with this wisdom. It does not increase in Buddhas, nor is it reduced in sentient beings. It is our fundamental nature, the essential reality of the universe; it is emptiness without self-nature. We should not fall into sameness which ignores distinctions, nor should we make distinctions that overlook sameness.

Dogen Zenji's teaching transcends small-minded notions. For him the precepts and Zen are identical; there is no difference. The precepts are simply the function of Bodhi-mind. When one has realized Bodhi-mind, one is the living Buddha-dharma, the manifestation of Buddha's precepts.

Transmitting the Buddha-dharma is the only way to maintain the living Wisdom of the Buddhas. Not to awaken to this Wisdom is killing the life of the Buddha. What worse crime could there be? This is not to say that stealing, lying, drinking alcohol, inappropriate sexual behavior, and so on, are of no consequence, but rather that the real intoxication is delusion. Self-clinging goes far beyond all other forms of indulgence. It is much worse to slander a single Bodhisattva or miss the opportunity to awaken even one person than it is to steal all the possessions of all sentient beings.

"Once the monks of the Eastern Hall and the Western Hall were disputing about a cat. Nansen, holding up the cat, said, 'Monks, if you can say a word of Zen, I will spare the cat. If you cannot, I will kill it!' No monk could answer. Nansen finally killed the cat."[2]

In the Maha Prajna expounded by Manjusri Bodhisattva, it says: "An ascetic who is pure and undefiled will not enter nirvana; a monk who breaks the precepts will not fall into hell."[3] How do you understand this? If you think that just by being a monk you can break the precepts and not suffer karmic consequences, you are in error; but if you think that by being pure and undefiled you will enter nirvana, you are gravely mistaken. However, if you have completely relinquished all dualistic thinking and abandoned home and country, then you may understand the meaning of this koan. If you do not understand it, then work on it with someone who does.

The continuity of the Buddha-dharma is impossible outside of the traditional context of face-to-face transmission. This means that self-appointed masters are unable to receive or transmit the true Dharma. Something would be lacking, something that only happens when one surrenders to the teaching through a vessel of the Dharma, a living Buddha.

The relationship with your teacher is the most important and complex relationship you can ever experience in life. It cannot be judged by ordinary social standards alone. You may try to evaluate and analyze whatever your teacher does and try to relate to that according to your own convictions, but you won't get very far. You may even end up more confused. Sometimes everything seems just how it should be, and at other times your expectations are not met at all. What is called for is a leap of faith. You have to let go of all your notions and take the teacher for what he or she is completely. This is called surrender and it has to be with a true master. You can only do it when you see your teacher as a living Buddha. Pema Chodron, a contemporary woman teacher in the Tibetan Buddhist tradition, recently said, "My personal teacher did not keep ethical norms and my devotion to him is unshakable."[4]

Master Engo says:

> The enlightened man enjoys perfect freedom in active life. He is like a dragon supported by deep waters or like a tiger that commands its mountain retreat. The man who is not enlightened drifts about in the affairs of the world. He is like a ram that gets its horns caught in a fence or like a man who waits for a hare to run against a tree stump and stun itself.
>
> The enlightened man's words are sometimes like a lion crouched to spring, sometimes like the Diamond King's treasure sword. Sometimes their effect is to shut the mouths of the world-famed ones, sometimes it is as if they simply follow the waves coming one after another. When the enlightened man meets others who are enlightened, then friend meets friend. He values them, and they encourage each other. When he meets those who are adrift in the world, then teacher meets disciple. His way of dealing with such people is far-sighted. He stands firm before them, like a thousand-fathom cliff.
>
> Therefore it is said that the Way of the absolute is manifest everywhere: it has no fixed rules and regulations. The teacher sometimes makes a blade of grass

stand for the golden-face Buddha, sixteen feet high, and sometimes makes the golden-face Buddha, sixteen feet high, stand for a blade of grass. Tell me, on what principle is all this based? Do you understand?[5]

It is impossible to realize what the Dharma is by groping and searching for it. When you try to grasp the Dharma, you always miss it. To give up your search altogether doesn't work either. How then do you realize the Dharma? This is a living koan. When you really seek the Way and exert yourself, completely forgetting everything, you find out that you were never separate from it. Then all questioning ceases. Those who have seen the Way forget their knowledge of it, transcending relative consciousness. How do you go beyond dualistic consciousness and overcome the illusion of being separate? Only through the practice of zazen. You cannot realize the Dharma without sitting and forgetting yourself. Without strong zazen practice you can do all kinds of good deeds but still miss the Way.

Eno lost his face [his deluded self] while training on Mount Huang-mei. The Second Patriarch, Eka, showed his earnestness by cutting off his arm in front of Bodhidharma's cave, realizing the Buddha-dharma through this action and turning his delusive mind into enlightenment. Thereafter he prostrated himself before Bodhidharma in deep respect before returning to his original position. Thus did he realize absolute freedom, dwelling in neither body nor mind, nonattached, unlimited.

In order to realize absolute freedom, the great matter of life and death has to be resolved. This is the most important thing one can accomplish in life and it is so precious that anybody who has attained this freedom can't help but urge others to do the same. Zen masters throughout the centuries went even so far as to use very rigorous *upaya*, expedient means, to bring about the awakening of their students. Bodhidharma stared at a wall for nine years waiting for someone to come along who was determined enough to go all the way. Finally Eka showed the right resolution, but he had to stand in the snow for a whole night and cut off his arm before Bodhidharma would even talk to him. Obaku beat Rinzai three times heartily without blinking an eye; Master Bokushu broke Ummon's leg; Tokusan gave thirty blows to anybody who dared to come close.

Of course these actions can't be generalized. They are direct responses to unique situations. Different students need different *upaya* and not all of us can deal with this kind of compassion. It depends on our karma as well as our capacity and resolve to seek the Way.

"The Transmission of the Lamp," *Keitoku Dento-roku*, gives us an impressive description of how the Second Patriarch Eka (Shinko) showed his eagerness in seeking the Truth and how he was first permitted to have *dokusan* with Bodhidharma:

> Shinko went over to Shorinji and day and night beseeched Bodhidharma for instruction. The Master always sat in zazen facing the wall and paid no attention to his entreaties. On the evening of December 9, heaven sent down a heavy snow. Shinko stood erect and unmoving. Toward daybreak the snow reached above his knees. The Master had pity on him and and said, "You have long been standing in the snow. What are you seeking?" Shinko in bitter tears said, "I beseech you, O Master, with your compassion pray open your gate of

Dharma and save all of us beings." The Master said, "The incomparable Truth of the Buddhas can only be attained by eternally striving, practicing what cannot be practiced and bearing the unbearable. How can you, with your little virtue, little wisdom, and with your easy and self-conceited mind, dare to aspire to attain the true teaching? It is only so much labor lost." Listening to the Master's admonition, Shinko secretly took out his sharp knife, himself cut off his own left arm, and placed it in front of the Master. The Master, recognizing his Dharma caliber, told him, "Buddhas, when they first seek after the Truth, give no heed to their bodies for the sake of Dharma. You have now cut off your arm before me. I have seen sincerity in your seeking."

The Master finally gave him the name Eka. Shinko asked, "Is it possible to listen to Buddha-dharma?" The Master replied, "The Buddha-dharma cannot be attained by following others." That is, one has to see directly into his own nature. Shinko said, "My mind is not yet at peace. I beg you, my teacher, please give it peace for me." Bodhidharma said, "Bring the mind to me, and I will set it at rest." The Second Patriarch said, "I have searched for the mind, and it is finally unattainable." Bodhidharma said, "I have thoroughly set it at rest for you."[6]

Going through the process of surrendering and becoming completely dependent is the prerequisite for mind-to-mind transmission. After the transmission of Buddha to Buddha, the student becomes a master and is independent. How he shows his gratitude and appreciation to his teacher, no matter what the teacher is like, shows whether the transmission was genuine or not. The whole transmission is about dropping all dualistic notions of good and evil and becoming One Mind.

A monk asked Joshu, "Does a dog have the Buddha-nature?" Joshu replied "Mu!" This word mu can be neither measured nor grasped, for there is nothing to grab hold of. I would suggest that you try letting go! Then ask yourself these questions: What are body and mind? What is Zen conduct? What are birth and death? What is the Buddha-dharma? What are worldly affairs? And what ultimately are mountains, rivers, and earth, or people, animals, and houses?

The question, "What is *mu*?" is often given to students as the first barrier of Zen. Dogen Zenji's advice is to fathom it as deeply as possible by letting go of all concepts, opinions, and preconceived ideas of what *mu* is. Then he tells us to turn our own light inward by asking ourself: "What are body and mind? What is Zen conduct? What are birth and death? What is the Buddha-dharma? What are worldly affairs?"

Whatever you grab hold of can't be "it." If you still try, you are still perceiving *mu* as an object separate from yourself. But *mu* stands for absolute reality and can't be cut. How can you cut the One? With what will the One be cut?

When you look into your own mind, you realize that there is no one that sees and there is nothing to be seen. Subject and object disappear. Any kind of division drops away. Working on *mu* means becoming one with it. Only then do you reveal your true face before your parents were born.

Dogen Zenji suggests that we try letting go; he shows his grandmotherly kindness. Just let go: the whole teaching comes down to this. Only your fear and self-doubt prevent you from doing it. In zazen this dilemma becomes paramount. Maybe you are too scared to jump, and yet holding on to your identity doesn't work either. It is painful and there is a yearning to go beyond your limited self.

In a way, time takes care of it. If you sit single-mindedly and wholeheartedly long enough, you will eventually get exhausted. With only so much strength, will, and stubbornness, sooner or later you must release your grip and fall. The amazing thing is that you do not lose anything. You might think you are losing your life, but only your attachment to body and mind is lost.

It is like a man up a tree who hangs from a branch by his mouth. His hands cannot grasp a bough and his feet cannot touch the tree. Another man comes under the tree and asks him the meaning of Bodhidharma's coming from the West. If he does not answer, he does not meet the questioner's need. If he answers, he will lose his life. At such a time, how should he answer?[7]

All you really lose is the concept of who you are. It may look as if you have to jump into a bottomless black hole, but after all it is just a small step, like stepping off the curb when you cross the street. So why not go ahead and just let go? There is no reason to put it off until tomorrow.

Dogen Zenji, the very founder of Soto Zen in Japan, gives us koan after koan to work on. What is mind? We talk about it all the time, but what is it? Is it just thoughts? Is it consciousness? Is it what we perceive or think? Or is it the thinker? Is it the one asking the questions or the one answering the questions? Does mind exist or not? Do I exist or not? When you try really hard to answer these questions and see with growing despair that all your efforts are in vain, body and mind will drop off. The only thing that holds you back is fear of losing your self.

The only ailment afflicting you is lack of faith in yourself. If you really trust, you can just let go of body and mind. Offer it up to the Buddha. Why bother holding onto it? After all, what are body and mind? What else but just this? Just this posture, just sitting, just this life itself. Whatever you do from morning until night is "it." Sitting, taking a walk, cooking, washing the dishes—each and every thing you do is nothing but the Way.

What is birth and what is death? If you look into your own mind, you can't find any birth or death. However hard this may be to accept, birth and death are only concepts of dualistic consciousness. You are being born and dying thousands of times each second. The whole body and all the particles composing it are constantly dying and being born. There is no fixed self to begin with, no entity called self. It is empty. All existence is just like this. Your true self-nature is no-self-nature.

What is the Buddha-dharma? Is it something apart from your life, apart from yourself, apart from this very body and mind? Our tendency to escape from reality is so strong that we cultivate that notion of separation endlessly. It is difficult to take life as it is, so you divide it up in different parts like body and mind, form and emptiness. It's all about keeping a safe distance. In zazen you return to the One. This form, this very body is empty, *mu* manifesting as form. Form is emptiness, emptiness is form; they are inseparable.

What are worldly affairs? All daily activities are just *mu* expressing itself as the functioning of this very body, which is the body of the Buddha. Everything you do from morning until night is nothing but the manifestation of Buddha-nature itself.

Even inanimate things are *mu*. It is interesting that Dogen Zenji includes houses. Buildings and institutions are empty to begin with, but we often treat them as indispensable. Maintaining the institution may even become more important than the practice itself. In speaking about right conduct for Zen monks, Dogen Zenji doesn't mention his temple Kosho-ji, or any other institution for that matter. And when Kosho-ji was threatened, he did not bother trying to protect it. He just left the temple for his enemies to burn down and went somewhere else with his students. The transmission of the true Dharma was more important to him than buildings and grounds.

If you continue to ask these questions, the two aspects—movement and nonmovement—will clearly not appear. This nonappearance, however, does not mean inflexibility. Unfortunately, however, very few people realize this, while many are deluded thereby. Zen trainees can realize this after they have trained for some time. It is my sincere hope, however, that you will not stop training even after you have become fully enlightened.

When you really pursue these questions in zazen, the two aspects, movement and nonmovement, just do not appear. This nonappearance is not a state of inflexibility, but quite the contrary, very dynamic and flowing. It goes beyond movement and stillness, and does not mean you should become a stone Buddha.

True Zen is always alive and dynamic, constantly changing, and can never be made into something solid and substantial. When you cling to your understanding, even if it comes out of your experience, the life of the Dharma is lost. You need to continuously return to the Source, which can never be grasped or fixated. If you really want to live it, you have to be flexible and flowing. How can you be an unmovable tree in a heavy wind? This has nothing to do with being rigid and inflexible, but rather with being solidly rooted in faith in the Dharma. True strength is not rigidity, but flexibility.

Unfortunately, however, very few people realize this, while many remain deluded. Zen students can come to realization after some period of training, but the point is not to stop sitting even after becoming fully enlightened. This is a vital matter, essential to the teaching. Many stop sitting after their first glimpse of enlightenment; some even begin teaching Zen.

A genuine realization of the truth can itself become a trap. It may give you the illusion that you can do whatever you want and still think that it is practice. Although zazen is not limited to sitting on a cushion, it is difficult to stay open and flexible without the sitting practice. One's understanding may become rigid and conceptual, just a memory of what was once fresh and alive.

Enlightenment is just the beginning. It is only when you realize there is nothing to attain that you can begin to practice true *shikantaza* (just sitting). This practice does not have awakening as a goal, but is rather practice-realization. With profound enlightenment, one realizes how much more there is still to accomplish. It is an endless process of refining one's life. Over and over again you will see things that were always right in front of your eyes, but went unnoticed because you were too self-involved.

With Bodhi-mind, your response to life situations becomes less mechanical. The right conduct Dogen Zenji advocates has nothing to do with any preconceived ideas about how things ought to be. These ideas only support self-righteousness and make you more rigid in your judgments. Every situation is absolutely unique and needs to be appreciated in that way. This calls for an open and flexible mind. In Zen, right and wrong are relative standards and right conduct is not governed by fixed rules.

Notes

1 Dogen Zenji, *Shobogenzo*, "Bendowa," translated by Nishiyama, Volume One, 147.
2 *Mumonkan*, Case 14, in Shibayama, 107.
3 Translated by Maezumi Roshi, unpublished.
4 From Pema Chodron's interview with Helen Tworkov in *Tricycle*, fall 1993, 21.
5 *Hekiganroku*, Case 8, Master Engo's Introduction, in Sekida, 168–69.
6 *Mumonkan*, Case 41, and Teisho on the koan, in Shibayama, 285–87.
7 *Mumonkan*, Case 5, in Shibayama, 53.

Points to Watch in Practicing the Way
Point Nine

The Need to Practice
in Accordance with the Way

*Buddhist trainees should first determine whether or not their
practice is headed toward the Way. Shakyamuni, who was able to
harmonize and control his body, speech, and mind, sat beneath a
bodhi tree doing zazen. Suddenly, upon seeing the morning star, he
became enlightened, realizing the highest supreme Way, which is
far beyond that of the sravakas and pratyekabuddhas. The
enlightenment that the Buddha realized through his own efforts has
been transmitted from Buddha to Buddha without interruption to
the present day. How, then, can those who have realized this
enlightenment not have become Buddhas? To be headed toward the
Way is to know its appearance and how far it extends. The Way
lies under the foot of every man. When you become one with the
Way you find that it is right where you are, thus realizing perfect
enlightenment. If, however, you take pride in your enlightenment,
even though it be very deep, it will be no more than partial enlight-*

enment. These are the essential elements of being headed toward the Way.

According to the Kegon sutra, at the moment of enlightenment Shakyamuni Buddha spontaneously cried out: "How wonderful! How wonderful! Intrinsically all sentient beings are the Buddha, endowed with the same wisdom and virtue as the Tathagata, but because men's minds have become inverted through delusive thinking, they fail to perceive this."

This is the essence of Zen Buddhism. What the Buddha means is that all human beings, whether male or female, young or old, sharp or dull, beautiful or plain, are whole and complete just as they are, that the nature of every being is inherently perfect without a flaw, no different from that of a Buddha.

Yet men and women, restless and anxious, live insecure lives because their minds, clouded by delusion, are turned upside down. What we need is to realize our original perfection and completeness, to see through the false picture of ourselves as incomplete and sinful, and to wake up to our inherent purity and wholeness.

The Buddha Tathagatas are those who have realized directly the unborn Buddha-mind. Intrinsically, each and every one and each and every thing is the Buddha. The Buddha Way is the highest Supreme Way, unexcelled and free from human agency. Nothing surpasses this Way and it cannot be altered by human beings.

The Buddha Shakyamuni transmitted the wondrous Dharma to Mahakasyapa through successive Patriarchs without alteration. The Dharma is the absolute Truth, which is universal, and no matter who realizes it—regardless of race, era, culture, age or gender—it is the same and never changes. It is the unchanging, undefiled *dharmakaya*, which is timeless and unalterable. This realization is confirming the highest Truth in oneself and is Supreme Enlightenment. It is known as *Annutara Samyak Sambodhi* and is the unsurpassed Wisdom of all the Buddhas.

This very Mind is the Buddha. It is transmitted by *jijuyu samadhi,* which means that an awakened one receives and uses the joy of awakening in himself. Buddhas realize and maintain it to awaken all beings in the three worlds. For Dogen Zenji *jijuyu samadhi* is zazen, the fundamental practice that includes both self-awakening and the awakening of all sentient beings. This is the zazen of dropped off body and mind, pure mirror-like *samadhi.* Everything is just what it is. By proper sitting in zazen one can enter this *jijuyu samadhi,* casting off body and mind.

Each and every person is complete and whole, not lacking even one degree of this Dharma, but unless one practices zazen it is not manifested, and unless there is realization it is not attained. Without realization, this Dharma, with which every person is amply endowed, cannot be attained and appreciated. It is not a question of one or many, good or bad, right or wrong; it transcends all duality. Let go of trying to grab it and it fills your whole being. It has no boundaries; it is without beginning or end.

When you speak of this Dharma, or you lift a hand or take a step, it is the same. In this *jijuyu samadhi* all Buddhas dwell as the Master. Nothing appears as separate from oneself. Becoming one with the Buddha Way is to find one's way through right effort. All dharmas exist within realization. With realization all dharmas appear as the Buddha-dharma. By going beyond enlightenment, one practices as a seamless Whole: no separation, no enlightenment, no delusion, no birth, no death—no such distinctions. When one goes beyond enlightenment and delusion, one is not affected by such apparent dualities or distinctions. One is free from suffering and confusion, beyond sanity and madness.

In the *Denkoroku,* "The Record of the Transmission of the Light," Keizan Zenji records a poem of the enlightenment of Micchaka Arya, the sixth Patriarch in India after the Buddha:

> Though we find clear waters ranging to the vast blue
> sky in autumn
> How can it compare with the hazy moon on a spring
> night!
> Most people want to have it pure white,
> But sweep as you will, you cannot empty the mind.[1]

This poem illustrates the most accomplished state of Zen. It also refers to the fact that most people want to become pure and perfect, but try as they will, it can't be done. The more you try to purify yourself, the more deluded you become. From the very beginning, you have always been intrinsically perfect, complete, and whole.

Trainees should first determine whether or not their practice is headed toward the Way. The more you try to gain something or become something else, the further astray you go. The most effective means to accomplish the Way is through zazen, just sitting with no goal.

From the very first time you sit down in the traditional posture of zazen, full and complete awakening is in realization. When you sit with deep faith in this fact, with the mind wholeheartedly involved in just sitting, then at some point you shall realize the truth of this statement.

The enlightenment that the Buddha realized through his own efforts has been transmitted from Buddha to Buddha without interruption to the present day. The lineage of the Buddhas and Patriarchs looks like a chain of individuals, but in fact it is one continuous pipeline transmitting the Dharma down through the ages and finally bringing it to us here now. Since it can only be handed down from Buddha to Buddha, one has to become a Buddha in order to transmit it. Although true teaching is difficult to find, fortunately there have always been individuals in every generation for the last twenty-five hundred years who have given their whole lives to making sure that the Dharma prevailed.

Even though everyone is complete and perfect to begin with, we don't always appear to be so perfect and complete. This is precisely why people go on trying to become pure and perfect, not realizing their intrinsic nature. An enlightened person, even though he realizes his intrinsic nature is complete and perfect, does not dwell there. For the sake of all sentient beings he descends the mountain of enlightenment and walks freely in the mud of the world.

Master Engo says: "Standing on the highest mountaintop, no devil or heretic can approach him. Descending to the farthest depths of the sea, he is not to be seen even by the Buddha's eyes. Even if your eye is like a shooting star and your spirit like lightning, you are still like the turtle, which cannot avoid dragging its tail. At such a juncture, what do you do?"[2]

How, then, can those who have realized this enlightenment not have become Buddhas? To be headed toward the Way is to know its appearance and how far it extends. The Way lies under the foot of everyone. You must realize what the Way is and how far it extends, whether it is long or short, high or low. What is the Buddha Way and where does it lead? When you are clear about the Way, the Way is always right where you stand; it is not a matter of far or near. When you truly realize enlightenment you are the Buddha.

When you become one with the Way you find that it is right where you are, thus realizing perfect enlightenment. Wherever you go is the Way. There is no chance of escape, because nothing exists apart from the Way; it is all-pervading and limitless.

However deep your enlightenment may be, if you take pride in it, it will be no more than partial enlightenment. When there is pride, there is still attachment to self. Once body and mind are dropped off, there is no fixation on self.

Present-day trainees strongly desire to see miracles, even though they do not understand how the Way functions. Who of these is not mistaken? They are like a child who, forsaking both his father and his father's wealth, runs away from home. Even though his father is rich, and he, as an only son, would someday inherit it all, he becomes a beggar, searching for his fortune in faraway places. This is truly the case.

Life itself is the priceless treasure. You are rich from the very beginning, so what is the point of going out to seek your fortune as if you were poor? Life provides everything you need, beyond scarcity and abundance. Only slow down and stop trying to accumulate more. The biggest miracle is this life itself. Why do you need to find any other miracles?

To study the Way is to try to become one with it—to forget even a trace of enlightenment. Those who would practice the Way should first of all believe in it. Those who believe in the Way should believe that they have been in the Way from the very beginning, subject to neither delusion, illusive thoughts, and confused ideas nor increase, decrease, and mistaken understanding. Engendering belief like this, clarify the Way and practice accordingly—this is the essence of studying the Way.

In studying the Way the point is to become one with the Way—to go far beyond all concerns about enlightenment and delusion. Why is it so difficult to be one with the Way? Why not let go of the attachment to your likes and dislikes? You create obstructions where there were none to begin with.

Koan study gives the opportunity to encounter all these obstructions directly, since it provides an almost endless series of problems. According to Shibayama Roshi, the best way to get a feel for the function of koans is to step in the shoes of a blind old lady. Imagine your cane is stolen, your dog is shot dead, and you are thrown down in the mud. Then you are beaten, spun around, and told to find your way home.[3]

The point of koans is not particularly to make practice any easier, and yet it is a most compassionate method. Koans can make life so difficult you give up resistance. Without struggle all obstructions vanish. If no one is fighting, the conflict is over. Being one with the barrier, you become the Way itself. By then you have no goal and no destination; therefore it is impossible to get lost. Wherever you are is the Way.

Yet if you don't realize this for yourself, it doesn't do you any good. From an absolute standpoint everything is the Way, but from the experiential side there is definitely a difference between being on the Way and going astray.

You forget the self when the mind is completely still. You sit in zazen and lose all sense of separation. There is no watcher or critic, no judge. "Me" disappears. In this there is not even a trace of anything. Where then is enlightenment? And what about "me"? When enlightenment is present, the self is no longer there. It is a nonexperience, because there is nobody to experience it and nothing to be experienced.

Those who would practice the Way should first of all believe in it. Faith is the foundation of practice. It is absolutely essential, not only in the beginning but all the way through. Those who hope for some final understanding that will make faith dispensable are going to be disappointed. They have it the wrong way around. The further you go, the less you understand and the more you rely on faith. Ultimately there is only faith.

The best way to cultivate faith is zazen. Sitting in *samadhi* gives you an opportunity to discover that nothing was ever lacking. There is no need for any belief system, concept, or person to make your life complete. Faith, even great faith, has always been present. It is just clouded over by the illusion that there is something lacking and something to be attained. Even enlightenment becomes a hindrance if that is what you become attached to.

In the beginning, in order to accomplish the Way you need to have faith in yourself, faith in your teacher, and faith in the practice of zazen. But in the end you need to have faith, not in anybody or anything, just faith. As notions and beliefs fade away, all you can do is trust. That is okay; after all, life has its own intelligence, its own wisdom.

Those who believe in the Way should believe that they have been in the Way from the very beginning, subject to neither delusion, illusive thoughts, and confused ideas nor increase, decrease, and mistaken understanding. To begin with, you always have been one with the Way. It is impossible to be outside it. The Way includes everything, even the notion that it doesn't include everything. Dropping that notion means admitting the Truth.

Why is it so hard to drop all notions and admit the Truth? Notions have no substance of their own and don't affect the Way by any means. Why do you put your trust in them and not in the Way itself? Why do you take ideas and concepts so seriously?

Clarify the Way and practice accordingly—this is the essence of studying the Buddha Way. Zazen turns your whole system upside down. It is absurd: losing ground, you gain faith. But faith is not solid and substantial. It is nothing—not the "nothing" of nihilism, but the creative and lively functioning of the Way. Nonbeing is far from nothing; it is beyond being and not being, as nonthinking is beyond thinking and not thinking. It is beyond all dualistic thinking. You learn to rely on that which is unborn and undying. To have faith in the Buddha-dharma is to have faith in oneself.

The second method of Buddhist training is to cut off the function of discriminating consciousness and turn away from the road of intellectual understanding. This is the manner in which novices should be guided. Thereafter they will be able to let body and mind fall away, freeing themselves from the dualistic ideas of delusion and enlightenment.

It is only by cutting the root of dualistic thinking that you can go beyond delusion and enlightenment. There is nothing wrong with discriminating mind, but we give it way too much power. We lose sight of the source and are bewildered by our own schemes. The only way home is in stopping the process, cutting off the root of discrimination. Then you'll find out that life and death are no different, that enlightenment is delusion and delusion enlightenment, that Buddhas and ordinary beings are one, that the Way is your life, and discriminating mind is Buddha-mind. It is all the same and yet different. How can this be? When you discriminate, you see these things as different; when you don't, they are not. As long as you see these things as different, you go on seeking nirvana and trying to escape samsara.

Dualistic thinking turns everything into concepts. I become a concept, you become a concept; life, death, practice, delusion, and enlightenment—all are nothing but concepts. In zazen you have a chance to break free by cutting off the functioning of discriminating consciousness. Thereafter you will be able to let body and mind fall away, freeing yourself from the dualistic ideas of delusion and enlightenment. If you remain attached to body and mind, you will never accomplish the Way. Only stop seeking after enlightenment and trying to get rid of delusion.

In general there are only a very few who believe they are in the Way. If only you believe that you are truly in the Way, you will naturally be able to understand how it functions, as well as the true meaning of delusion and enlightenment. Make an attempt at cutting off the function of discriminating consciousness; then, suddenly, you will have almost realized the Way.

There have always been very few who trust they are in the Way. You are the Way, but have you confirmed this for yourself? If you would only trust that you are the Way itself, you would naturally be able to appreciate how it functions as well as to grasp the true meaning of delusion and enlightenment. You should make a serious attempt to cut off the function of discriminating mind; then, suddenly, you will have almost realized the Way.

Since it is difficult to cut off discriminating consciousness all at once, most often your efforts will result in brief glimpses of the Way. The effect can be compared to the working of a camera lens. It opens for a moment and almost immediately shuts again. Over time, practice will open the lens for longer and longer periods until the shutter does not close anymore. Finally the Buddha is completely revealed; one sees with the same eyes and hears with the same ears as all the Buddhas. By realizing one's essential nature and receiving the Dharma Seal of Transmission, one becomes the living Buddha-Patriarch, giving birth to all the Buddhas and Patriarchs.

Notes

[1] Keizan Zenji, *Denkoroku*, Case 6.

[2] *Hekiganroku*, Case 24, Master Engo's Introduction, in Sekida, 210.

[3] Adapted from Teisho on *Mumonkan*, Case 13, Shibayama, 101.

Points to Watch in Practicing the Way
Point Ten

The Direct Realization of the Way

There are two ways to realize enlightenment. One is to train under a true Zen master, listening to his teaching; the other is to do zazen single-mindedly. In the former case you give full play to the discriminating mind, while through the latter, practice and enlightenment are unified. To enter the Way neither of these two methods can be dispensed with.

There are two ways to realize enlightenment, but they should not be seen as separate. To practice zazen single-mindedly with one's whole heart and to study under the guidance of a true master are both absolutely essential. When you train under a master and listen to his teaching, you have the opportunity to put personal views and preconceptions aside. In zazen, body and mind, practice and enlightenment are unified. To enter the Way neither of these two methods can be dispensed with. Without the guidance of a true teacher you may go completely astray. Without doing zazen single-mindedly you may end up with only deluded understanding, dualistic and shallow.

Someone without true realization, and lacking confirmation by an authentic teacher, can easily fall into the delusion that long study alone is sufficient to teach Zen, and may influence others to accept dualistic ideas about practice. This is truly regrettable, for this way people are robbed of the opportunity to really accomplish their life as the life of the living Buddha.

Some people actually believe that it is enough to just sit and not study intimately with a true teacher. There are others who study with a teacher but do not devote themselves single-mindedly to zazen. Both are far from the Way and fall short of transmitting the true Dharma.

Zazen prepares the ground for receiving the teaching so you learn to listen, not just with your ears but with your whole body and mind. Then during extended periods of sitting, things begin to settle and are slowly digested. This opens the mind to allow more teaching to enter. It is a kind of osmosis.

Just hearing words is not enough. The teaching goes beyond what could ever be said. You need to absorb it through the pores of your skin. The closer you work with a true teacher the greater the opportunity there is for this to happen. When you listen to a Dharma talk, you must sit in zazen with whole body and mind. When you receive the teaching only through your head, it is obstructed by too many opinions and ideas and cannot penetrate to the heart.

True Zen masters may wish to give the teaching to everyone, but not everyone is able to receive it. All students put up barriers at some point and remain attached to their own views. The more correct these views seem to be, the harder they are to let go of. People who hold tight to their opinions can never attain the Way. Your capacity to receive the teaching is greatly determined by your willingness to continuously let go and open up.

Great teachers are often demanding. They have to be; it comes out of their compassion. The true Dharma needs very tenacious characters in order to survive. It is said in Zen that lion cubs are pushed into a ravine by their mother not long after birth. Only the ones that make it back to the top will she care for and feed. They have proven to be strong enough to become king of the jungle and carry on the species. Transmitting the Dharma is something like that.

Everyone is endowed with body and mind, though their actions inevitably vary, being either strong or weak, brave or cowardly. It is through the daily actions of your body and mind, however, that you directly become enlightened. This is known as the realization of the Way.

Everyone has a body and a mind, and is therefore capable of receiving the Dharma. Essentially there is no difference between ordinary people and Buddhas. The only distinction is attachment to the notion of self. There are no Buddhas apart from sentient beings and no sentient beings apart from Buddhas, just as there is no ice apart from water and no water apart from ice.

Buddha-nature is comparable to free-flowing water. Most people don't experience that kind of freedom because self-clinging has made them solid and stuck, as if they were frozen. No wonder relationships don't always run smoothly. And yet no great change is required to be completely fluid and free. You don't have to become anything other than yourself. Just by letting go of the illusion of self, you dissolve and return to your essential nature. At that moment, you realize that all your everyday actions are the expression of Buddha. Brushing your teeth, combing your hair, putting on clothes, eating food, doing your work are all Buddha's activities. So tell me, where is Buddha when you go shopping? Where is Buddha when you are driving your car?

There is no need to change your existing body and mind, for the direct realization of the Way simply means to become enlightened through training under a true Zen master. To do this is neither to be bound by old viewpoints nor to create new ones; it is simply to realize the Way.

Direct realization of the Way simply means to drop off body and mind and attain realization under an authentic Zen master. To do this is neither to be attached to your old viewpoints nor to create new ones; it is simply to realize the Way. Just be your ordinary Self. All efforts to change, improve, or adjust are useless in the end. Body and mind can never really settle if you continually stir things up with your dissatisfaction.

Water that is cloudy can only turn clear when it is left quiet. The dirt will settle to the bottom of its own accord. Any attempt to force this to happen must fail. The same is true in zazen. Only when body and mind sit completely still, self forgotten, can the mind return to its original pure and clear nature. Random thoughts are not the problem if they are simply allowed to come and go freely. It is dualistic and conceptual thinking that continues to stir up the mind.

Fighting confusion with more thoughts doesn't help; you only end up exhausted. To continually discriminate requires a great deal of effort. We are so used to it that we don't always notice, but thinking depends on the effort you put into it. If you stop providing fuel, the whole process slows down. Thinking will cease and the mind will settle by itself. The only solution is just to sit stably in *samadhi* and think of not-thinking. How do you think of not-thinking? Beyond thinking. This is the essential way of zazen.

For the direct realization of the Way, neither be bound by old viewpoints nor create new ones. No fixed perspective will ever be sufficient, because mind and all phenomena are in constant flux. All efforts to evaluate, judge, and criticize, even with the best of intentions, are nothing but a means to avoid accepting the teaching and realizing the Way.

It's easy enough to be critical. In one sense, no one is perfect, not even a Buddha. Your teacher is no exception. You will always find flaws: he or she is too young or too old, too strict or too loose, too humble or too arrogant, too distant or too intimate, too wild or too boring. If you are caught up in your own judgments, you miss that which is most precious, the opportunity to relinquish the self.

In the sutra, *Identity of Relative and Absolute*, it says, "Do not judge by any standards." In order to judge at all, standards are needed. If you don't judge, you don't need standards.

Gakudo Yojinshu means "Points to Watch in Practicing the Way." There are so many ways to practice zazen. You need to be clear as to how to proceed or you will go completely astray. Without dropping off body and mind you cannot be one with the Way. Not at peace with yourself, you will continue to suffer.

Of course pain can never be avoided, but it does not

necessarily have to turn into suffering. In fact, being at one with your pain leads to the end of all suffering. That is probably why no one has ever been able to attain the Way without going through great difficulty. It is only through experiencing your own pain that you can clarify the Way and identify with the suffering of all sentient beings. If you hold back and resist, true wisdom and compassion cannot arise.

In Zen, training is often compared to the forging of a sword. Its strength and sharpness depend on the process it goes through. The sword gets plunged into the fire until it is red hot, struck with a hammer, cooled down in water, then put back into the fire and beaten again, over and over. As the sword becomes more tempered, the beating gets more refined. Endless practice means endlessly refining your life.

Master Engo says: "The words which command the universe are obeyed throughout the ages. The spirit able to quell the tiger amazes even thousands of holy ones. His words are matchless, his spirit prevails everywhere. If you want to go through with your advanced training, you must enter the great master's forge. Tell me, who could ever show such spirit?"[1]

Notes

[1] *Hekiganroku*, Case 42, Master Engo's Introduction, in Sekida, 265.

Yuibutsu Yobutsu

Only Buddha and Buddha

Only Buddha and Buddha
Part One
—··—··—··—··—◈—··—··—··—··—

Buddha-dharma cannot be known by a person. For this rea-
son, since olden times no ordinary person has realized Buddha-
dharma; no practitioner of the Lesser Vehicles has mastered
Buddha-dharma. Because it is realized by Buddhas alone, it is said,
"Only a Buddha and a Buddha can thoroughly master it."

Buddha-dharma cannot be known by an ordinary person. This means that a person with deluded understanding
cannot know intimately the Buddha-dharma. Only one who
has cut off the root of dualistic thinking and who has awakened Bodhi-mind can know the true Buddha-dharma. It cannot be realized by anyone who practices the Lesser Vehicle
(Hinayana). We should not confuse Hinayana with
Theravadan Buddhism. Hinayanists have their own liberation
as a goal rather than that of all beings. They adhere to a narrow and literal interpretation of the Dharma, putting more
emphasis on words and letters and rules and regulations than

133

they do on *prajna* wisdom. They can be found in any tradition, including Zen.

As long as you are afraid of confusion and always look for clarity, adhering strictly to rules and regulations, words and letters, you will not realize the Buddha-dharma. With that kind of insecurity it is difficult to accept the reality of life. Clarifying the Dharma means admitting that life is groundless. Whatever is born must die. There isn't anything lasting or fixed. You might try giving your life a solid foundation by adhering to a doctrine or an ideology, but you only succeed in deceiving yourself.

Your notions about how a Buddha should appear can stand in the way of recognizing a Buddha when you actually meet one. Shakyamuni Buddha once asked Subhuti, one of his closest disciples, if he believed that Buddha had the thirty-two marks mentioned in the scriptures. Subhuti replied that precisely not having these thirty-two marks meant having the marks of the Buddha. The World-honored One then uttered this verse:

> Who sees me by form,
> Who seeks me in sound,
> Perverted are his footsteps upon the Way;
> For he cannot perceive the Tathagata.[1]

So if you are looking for somebody special, you will find all sorts of saints, but no Buddha. Then you are stuck, because only a Buddha can transmit to a Buddha. The Buddha-dharma is only realized by Buddhas alone. It is only transmitted from Buddha to Buddha. An ordinary person cannot transmit the Buddha-dharma and a Buddha cannot transmit to an ordinary person. Only Buddha to Buddha.

All Buddhas, awakened people, have the ability to realize complete enlightenment and transmit this enlightenment from one to another without deviation. This ability goes beyond any human devices and is not bound by them; it is transmitted by *jijuyu samadhi*. This is the right method and only standard of transmission from Buddha to Buddha.

When you realize Buddha-dharma, you do not think, "This is realization just as I expected." Even if you think so, realization invariably differs from your expectation. Realization is not like your conception of it. Accordingly, realization cannot take place as previously conceived. When you realize Buddha-dharma, you do not consider how realization came about. You should reflect on this: What you think one way or another before realization is not a help for realization.

Bodhi-mind can never be conceived of; whatever you imagine it to be, it is never that, for Bodhi-mind can never be imagined or conceived. It is as if someone who was blind from birth were suddenly given the power of sight. No matter how hard such a person might have tried beforehand to visualize, it still would have been impossible.

All ideas about enlightenment are useless. The "good" ones are no better than the "bad" ones. Trusting in any of them is delusion. Imagine you have some beautiful notion of what enlightenment is and what enlightened behavior must look like, and then you try hard to conform to this model. You'll end up putting on an act all day long. There is no particular behavior or mannerism that could strictly be called enlightened.

No one needs to imitate anybody. Each one of us is perfect as we are. Even our flaws are part of our beauty. That is what you need to realize for yourself. How this realization will manifest in your life no one can predict.

To awaken Bodhi-mind is to discover the most profound treasure, one that nobody could have ever imagined existed. This is precisely why the drive and desire to share awakening with all beings arises so strongly. It is as if we had been going a hundred miles an hour in the wrong direction and suddenly turned about. Up to that moment we have been pursuing position, fame and profit; suddenly we realize in an instant that we have been living in a dream, that these pursuits are completely empty and meaningless.

When you awaken to Bodhi-mind you realize that nothing is permanent, graspable, or certain, and that all attempts to gain security and profit are meaningless. The only thing with meaning is to awaken all beings from this dream. It is the driving force that motivates an awakened person. All other interests drop away. All other desires lose their hold on you.

Preconceptions are barriers to realization. In fact, even having heard that enlightenment is possible becomes an obstacle. The Buddha Shakyamuni should have been stifled the moment he opened his mouth. He has created an immense problem for generations of descendants. All great masters are just like this, creating problems where none have existed, concocting medicine where there has never been any illness.

When you awaken Bodhi-mind and realize Buddha, you do not consider how this realization came about. There is no way of knowing all the karmic factors that brought about such a profound awakening. One can only speculate as to the reasons. A quantum leap is involved. Whatever you were thinking the Way to be was really of no significance. Realization happens not through your intention or wish, but in spite of yourself. It is always a spontaneous awakening that has little to do with you.

Although realization is not like any of the thoughts preceding it, this is not because such thoughts were actually bad and could not be realization. Past thoughts in themselves were already realization. But since you were seeking elsewhere, you thought and said that thoughts cannot be realization.

Just because realization does not conform to your preconceptions, it does not mean that preconceived ideas and understanding are inherently bad. There is nothing wrong with having ideas or concepts, only that they are a barrier to enlightenment when you cling to them. In order for Bodhi-mind to awaken, there must be an empty vessel. You can only become empty when you are not able to sort everything out in the way you would like to and your mind reaches an impasse. Only when you can neither step forward nor retreat, being totally blocked and desperate, can body and mind drop off. Whatever happens has nothing to do with what you may have been trying to figure out. Your very thoughts and ideas themselves are nothing but realization, Bodhi-mind; but since you were searching in the wrong direction, you couldn't realize that the very thoughts and words you were expressing were nothing less than Buddha's wisdom. Everything that flows out of your heart is the Buddha-dharma. It is only because of your dualistic perception that you do not realize this.

Whenever you seek after enlightenment, it will elude you. In fact, when you direct yourself toward it, you go away from it. But even this can turn into a concept and give you the wrong impression that, since you can't direct yourself toward it, it is wiser just to wait for enlightenment. Someone who decides to wait may wait for a very long time.

There is nothing unnatural about enlightenment, but it never happens without great effort. Only by dropping your preconceived notions can you awaken. For this you need to study with a truly compassionate teacher who is willing to destroy all your notions.

You should know that neither enlightenment nor delusion exist. From the beginning there has never been such a thing as delusion or enlightenment. They are just concepts—tentative terms without substance. A tree is a tree; it has no concept of whether it is enlightened or deluded. Only human beings have such foolish notions.

However, it is worth noticing that what you think one way or another is not a help for realization. Then you are cautious not to be small-minded. If realization came forth by the power of your prior thoughts, it would not be trustworthy. Realization does not depend on thoughts, but comes forth far beyond them; realization is helped only by the power of realization itself. Know that then there is no delusion, and there is no realization.

It is very important to realize that whatever you think is of no help toward realization. Don't be caught up in petty and small-minded views; they will only keep you bound and deluded. Small-mindedness can never bring you to the great joy of complete liberation and the free functioning of one who has gone beyond all notions of good and evil.

From the very beginning you were never deluded. Any realization that could arise through the power of your own thoughts would not be the true realization. Realization does not depend on thoughts, ideas, or beliefs. It is only realization itself which brings about realization. When Bodhi-mind is awakened, you awaken to the Truth that there is no realization to be attained and no delusion to begin with. There is no dust to be wiped off. The mind is like vast empty space. Nothing can disturb it; nothing can stick to it.

Notes

[1] Price and Wong. *The Diamond Sutra & The Sutra of Hui-neng* (Boston: Shambhala, 1990), 47.

Only Buddha and Buddha
Part Two

When you have unsurpassed wisdom, you are called Buddha. When a Buddha has unsurpassed wisdom, it is called unsurpassed wisdom. Not to know what it is like on this path is foolish. What it is like is to be unstained. To be unstained does not mean that you try forcefully to exclude intention or discrimination, or that you establish a state of nonintention. Being unstained cannot be intended or discriminated at all.

Anyone who has awakened the Bodhi-mind has unsurpassed wisdom and is a Buddha. This unsurpassed wisdom is also known as *prajna*, the wisdom that goes beyond dualistic thinking. It is transcendental and beyond good and evil, enlightened and deluded, Buddhas and sentient beings.

It is sad that not everyone awakens to Bodhi-mind. To pursue other goals such as fame and profit, or to favor fixed notions about right and wrong, is foolish. The Bodhi-mind is unstained and unsurpassable. This does not mean that intention or discrimination should be excluded. Sometimes it is important to acknowledge differences and just make a choice. Sometimes it is necessary to make great effort and, however difficult, just to do what needs to be done. And yet, intention and discrimination do not affect the Mind whatsoever. The Mind is pure and undefiled and can never be stained.

Being unstained is like meeting a person and not considering what he looks like. Also it is like not wishing for more color or brightness when viewing flowers or the moon.

Looking at people, we often don't see them. You may think you do, but in fact you don't; all you are facing is your pictures and ideas. Being unstained is like seeing people exactly for what they are without trying to have them live up to your own expectations. This gives them the space to just be themselves.

To experience unconditional and complete acceptance is liberating and empowering for everyone, but most people are afraid of this freedom and power because of the responsibility it involves. One has to practice for a very long time and go through many hardships and disappointments just in order to see a chair as a chair and a table as a table. Most difficult is just to see a person as a person without preconceptions, opinions, and judgments. Only by dropping all notions are you able to see things that way. Then, when you look at the moon and flowers, it is just the moon and flowers you see, not some distorted picture created to conform to a preconceived idea. Anything and everything can be seen just as it is. When you really are looking, you are completely one with what you are seeing, without any gap between subject and object.

Spring has the tone of spring, and autumn has the scene of autumn; there is no escaping it. So when you want spring or autumn to be different from what it is, notice that it can only be as it is. Or when you want to keep spring or autumn as it is, reflect that it has no unchanging nature.

Even though change in the seasons and within nature itself is inevitable, some do not accept this and try to avoid it. The unawakened cannot experience and accept all things as they are, because life is sometimes painful and frightening. Even though there are many things in life that are inevitable, they continue to pick and choose, accepting what they like and rejecting what they dislike. The awakened know no difficulty; they simply are not attached to their preferences.

When Dogen Zenji talks about appreciating spring and autumn, he is not only suggesting that you honor the seasons as they come; he is stressing the importance of accepting oneself and others without reservation. Only the foolish try to make everything and everyone conform to their preferences. Whether or not you like winter, when it is cold you are cold. Whether or not you enjoy summer, when it is hot you are hot. Your likes and dislikes are of no relevance whatsoever. Holding on to preferences only creates suffering for yourself and others.

When you are caught up in getting ahead in the world, it is easy to forget how to be satisfied. There is always a desire for more; but a new home or a better car, a different lover or more money will not stop the craving. So why not take things as they are? When it is spring, appreciate spring; when it is fall, appreciate fall. If you are thin, just be thin; if you are fat, just be fat. Some of you are fast, others slow; some are intelligent, others less so. What could be more natural?

In zazen you have a chance to see things just as they are, and the smallest glimpse is already a miracle. Even the most accurate description of it would not have come close to conveying the genuine experience. Most people are so conditioned to striving and fighting in order to get their lives together that it comes as a shock to see that there was never any problem to begin with. You are inherently perfect and complete. It's just your dualistic thinking and endless manipulation that is causing all the trouble.

Everything is changing continuously, but it is useless to cling to the way it was and to resist what is coming next. Some even fear their own mind because it is so unpredictable: happy yesterday, depressed today, what will it be tomorrow? In zazen you generate the power to sit still and face whatever wants to surface. Dark and ominous clouds may appear, but your initial fear will subside as you discover that none of them have any substance. If you realize who you really are, you find you're unfixed and constantly changing. Each of you is the undefiled and unchanging *dharmakaya*.

Zuigan asked Ganto, "What is the unchanging *dharmakaya*, everlasting reality?" Ganto said, "It has moved." Zuigan asked, "How about when it moves?" Ganto said, "Then you can't see the everlasting reality." Zuigan considered this a moment. Ganto said, "If you affirm this, you are not rid of the root of defilement. If you do not affirm it, you are immersed in endless birth and death."[1]

Nishiyama translated Dogen Zenji's words in a slightly different way: "Experience spring as spring and autumn as autumn. Accept the beauty and loneliness of both. Even though change in the seasons and within nature itself is inevitable, some do not accept this, and try, by all means available, to avoid it. The pure in heart, however, do not isolate these thoughts, but realize them also to be part of themselves. One may falsely believe that it is oneself that hears the birds sing in spring, and sees the leaves fall in autumn. This is not so."[2]

The pure in heart do not isolate anything, but realize everything to be aspects of mind. Jesus said, "Blessed are the pure in heart for they will see God."[3] For Dogen Zenji, those who have a pure heart will realize that everything that arises—thoughts, feelings, the sounds of birds, the sight of falling leaves—is nothing but the unchanging *dharmakaya*. He says somewhere, all sounds are nothing but the voice of my little Shakya, meaning that everything is nothing but the Buddha. Buddha and oneself are not seen as two.

Nothing exists outside Mind. Everything that appears in your thoughts is Mind itself. This Mind is all-pervading. All dharmas, all things, all phenomena—all are nothing but Mind.

"One may falsely believe that it is oneself that hears the birds sing in spring, and sees the leaves fall in autumn. This is not so." There is no self to hear and no self to see. There is only just hearing, just seeing. There is only the function of hearing, the function of seeing. If one thinks that there is something that hears and sees, one is gravely mistaken. You must look through this delusion and realize what no-self is. This very Mind is Buddha.

Kanzeon attained enlightenment just by hearing the sounds of the world. If you turn your light inward, then you will realize what hears the sounds. It is the One Buddha-mind, which is unborn and undying.

What is this One Mind? It is no other than your life as it unfolds from moment to moment. But somehow it is difficult to accept spring as spring, fall as fall, yourself as yourself.

Those who are not aware of the fact that they are perfect already are constantly trying to become better. All their attempts are doomed to fail. There is no practice, no Way, no Buddha, no Dharma, no enlightenment, no delusion.

That which is accumulated is without self, and no mental activity has self. The reason is that not one of the four great elements or the five skandhas *can be understood as self or identified as self, even though you think it is self. Still, when you clarify that there is nothing to be disliked or longed for, then the original face is revealed by your practice of the way.*

Whatever you accumulate—money, power, position— all is empty and without substance. No matter how much we cling, we cannot prevent anything from coming and going. Whatever is born must die. What you have today may be gone tomorrow. Children leave home and those we love can become foes; wealth, prestige, and power can be lost.

All mental activity is without self, as are all dharmas. The five *skandhas* are altogether empty and without self. Turning your own light inward and illuminating the self, you realize this self-nature is no-self, which is your True Self. Since all things are unfixed, you are already completely liberated. This samsaric world of suffering is already the world of liberation. There is nothing to be done and no one to do it. The great universe is one and can't be divided into enlightenment and delusion. It is a waste of time to even try to understand or control it. The universe is beyond anyone's comprehension or control. When you drop all understanding and clarify that there was never anything to hate or to cherish, your original face before your parents were born is revealed.

Notes

[1]*Shoyuroku*, unpublished translation by Yamada Koun and Robert Aitken.
[2]Nishiyama, volume three, 130.
[3]Mitchell, 158.

Only Buddha and Buddha
Part Three

A teacher of old said: Although the entire universe is nothing but the Dharma body of the self, you should not be hindered by the Dharma body. If you are hindered by the Dharma body, you will not be able to turn freely, no matter how hard you may try. But there should be a way to be free from hindrance. If you cannot say clearly how to free all people, you will soon lose even the life of the Dharma body and sink in the ocean of suffering for a long time.

Here Dogen Zenji is concerned that one might get attached to the One Body and be blinded by the _dharmakaya_. When you cast away the self, you become the Dharma. When you cast away the Dharma, you become yourself.

Zen practice is to forget oneself and become the Buddha-dharma. Then you must throw out the Buddha-dharma, kill all the Buddhas and Patriarchs, and be completely yourself. The true Master has experienced his complete aloneness and does not rely on anyone else's confirmation.

The entire universe and your life are inseparable. Your life is completely dependent on all dharmas and all dharmas are not apart from your life. The entire universe is the Dharma body, the true body of the self. You should not be hindered by it. If you are, you will not be able to turn freely. It is precisely because the entire body is empty of self that you are already enlightened and free. Without doing anything you are already liberated. This is why there is nothing to attain.

Those who do not realize Bodhi-mind are unable to awaken sentient beings; therefore they lose the life of the Dharma body and will eventually sink into endless suffering. If you wish to realize complete freedom and actualize the Way of the Buddhas, you must do your utmost to clarify this matter.

If you are asked in this way, how can you answer so as to keep the Dharma body alive and avoid sinking in the ocean of suffering?

In that case, say, "The entire universe is the Dharma body of the self." When you say that the entire universe is the Dharma body of the self, words cannot express it. When words cannot express it, should we understand there is nothing to be said? Without words, ancient Buddhas said something.

Words can never express the realization of the Buddha, but if you cannot express it, then your awakening is still unclear. It is the practice of a Bodhisattva to express the inexpressible and free those from suffering who are already free. The Buddha taught every day for forty-nine years and never spoke a word. There have been Buddha-Patriarchs for twenty-five hundred years, and yet not a single word has been uttered. The Buddha Shakyamuni's holding up a flower is the clear and profound teaching of "not a single word has been expressed." Mahakasyapa's smile is the proof that not a single teaching has been given. There has not been a single Dharma transmitted, nor did Bodhidharma ever come from the West. Shakyamuni Buddha never died and Maitreya will never be born.

> Lonely and deep, in the cloudy valley,
> Still the sacred pine tree
> Has passed through the cold of many years.[1]

There is birth in death, and there is death in birth. Death is entirely death, and birth is entirely birth. This is so not because you make it so, but because Dharma is like this. Therefore, when Buddha turns the Dharma wheel, there is insight such as this and expression such as this. Know that it is also like this when Buddha manifests a body to awaken sentient beings. This is called "awareness of no-birth."

There is death in birth and there is birth in death. When you drop your dualistic consciousness, you realize that birth and death are not two. Because all things are being born and dying eighty-four thousand times a second, you are already liberated. All things are Buddha-dharma; therefore everything is unfixed and constantly in flux. For this reason life does not become death and death does not become life. Life is absolute in itself and death is absolute in itself. Death is entirely death and life is entirely life. When it is time to live, just live; when it is time to die, just die. It has nothing to do with your effort or intention, but because the Buddha-dharma is just like this. It is for this reason that, when one has awakened to Bodhi-mind, there is realization and expression.

Only when you realize Bodhi-mind completely do you know for sure that nothing is fixed, that everything is continuously in flux. Then you have no longer any fear of death or what happens after death. The fear that ordinary people experience comes from not having awakened to Bodhi-mind. They somehow don't really acknowledge the Truth, so there is a fear of falling into either eternal hell or eternal nothingness. For those who have awakened to Bodhi-mind, there is nothing to fear because nothing is permanent. An eternal hell is created by not recognizing and confirming the Truth of impermanence. The thought that one could be locked up in hell for all eternity, that there is something fixed without the possibility of escape, is unbearable.

Nirvana, or liberation, is the realization that life and death are not fixed. The fact that everything is ungraspable is the liberation. We are constantly liberated because we cannot hold onto anything. This is continuous *satori*. It is not about understanding anything.

Everyone adjusts to any situation they find themselves in, even to starvation, AIDS, cancer, or the death of loved ones. This ability to adjust is Buddha-nature, which is no-self-nature, no fixed self, nothing permanent.

Although most of us have lots of ideas about life and death, in fact we cannot live before we've died. Until we've completely died to the self, we can't be called truly alive. Only the experience of death can show us how to live. The problem is that everybody wants to live but no one wants to die. Is there anyone who would undergo the experience of dying the same death and living the same life as the Buddha?

Dai kensho, true enlightenment, is the "great death." After total surrender, your life is just the life of Buddha-dharma. It is death within death, because something dies that never really existed to begin with, your small self, or ego. It is life within life because you realize that your very life is the life of Buddha-dharma. It brings up tremendous compassion and the desire to awaken others.

The Buddha Shakyamuni, when teaching the Dharma, spoke of life and death as one, the ultimate Truth: this is the experience of nonduality. Life is death and death is life. They are absolutely one. *Samsara* is nirvana: in the midst of pain and suffering is great liberation. No matter how you understand, appreciate, or actually live your life, reality is right here. It is nothing else but this.

When a Buddha is awakened, sentient beings are liberated, for there are no sentient beings apart from Buddhas and no Buddhas apart from sentient beings. And yet Buddhas are precisely Buddhas and sentient beings are ordinary people. When you realize enlightenment, you realize that there are no Buddhas and no sentient beings, no enlightenment and no delusion, no self and no others; but the Buddha Way goes beyond such understanding. There are Buddhas and ordinary people, enlightenment and delusion, life and death. With our attachment flowers fall, and weeds spring up with our aversion.

When a Buddha manifests a body, it is only for the purpose of awakening sentient beings. For this reason it is called no-birth. When an ordinary being awakens to the awareness of no-birth, he is called a Buddha. All the great Buddha-Patriarchs were just like this. None of them clung to their old views of good and evil, right and wrong. They freed themselves and others from birth and death and from endless suffering. They were no longer attached to their own bodies and minds, let alone the bodies and minds of others. When it was time to use the killing sword of Manjusri, they did not blink an eye or hesitate for an instant. When it was time to give life, they gave it freely and without restraint. They never put as much as a single barrier between themselves and others out of fear of losing their own lives or reputations. This is precisely the reason that in this decadent age we still have the Buddha-dharma to practice and to realize. If it weren't for these great Buddha-Patriarchs, who gave no thought to their own lives, we would not have the true spirit of Dogen Zenji to appreciate today.

"Buddha manifests a body and awakens sentient beings" means that awakening sentient beings is itself the manifestation of the Buddha body. In the midst of awakening sentient beings, do not pursue manifestation. Seeing manifestation, do not look about for awakening.

Awakening sentient beings is itself the manifestation of the Buddha body. When you cling to yourself and your own opinions of right and wrong, you manifest the body of a deluded person. With one moment of awakening, Buddha appears; with a single dualistic thought, an ordinary sentient being is revealed. Do you want to go on endlessly transmigrating in the three worlds, not even able to liberate yourself, no less the self of others? If you are a student of the Way, you should reflect on this.

It is as a result of awakening sentient beings that the *dharmakaya* emerges in the form of the actual body of the Buddha. Buddha appears for the sole purpose of awakening sentient beings; for no other purpose does Buddha appear. *Dharmakaya*, or One Body, emerges as the actual body of the

Buddha when it is involved in awakening sentient beings. But *dharmakaya* cannot appear as the body of Buddha if this body and mind are already filled. If you are full of opinions and ideas, then there is no room for anything else. When you empty yourself and dedicate your life to awakening sentient beings, this very body becomes the life of the Buddha.

In the midst of awakening sentient beings, do not look for characteristics and manifestations of the Buddha. The Buddha's characteristics are no characteristics, as the Buddha's activity is nonactivity. Buddha appears according to the necessity for liberating sentient beings. Buddha has no particular manifestation. Buddha may appear enlightened to Buddhas, and Buddha may appear deluded to ordinary people.

The ultimate point of the Buddha-dharma is liberation for oneself and others. When one realizes enlightenment, what arises is Bodhi-mind, the wish to awaken all sentient beings. Every time a Buddha appears, it is for this purpose alone. Being awakened and awakening others is the very nature and manifestation of the Buddha.

Understand that in the midst of awakening sentient beings, the Buddha-dharma is totally experienced. Explain it and actualize it this way. Know that it is the same with manifestation and having the Buddha body.

The Buddha-dharma is totally manifested in the midst of awakening sentient beings. All Buddha's activity is for the sole purpose of awakening sentient beings and bringing them to the great liberation of the Buddha Tathagata. When ordinary people perceive this functioning, they are confused and distressed. They do not understand the great benevolent compassion of Master Tokusan's Thirty Blows or of Obaku's. They see such functioning only through their dualistic mind, clinging to their own ideas of right and wrong.

A Buddha can actualize nothing else but Buddha-dharma. All the activities and actions of the Buddha are Dharma. A Buddha-Patriarch cannot separate what is Dharma from what is ordinary activity. Everything is Buddha-dharma. Ordinary people want to know if the activity comes from self or from no-self. Unless they drop such dualistic notions, they will never be able to liberate themselves, let alone others.

This is so because "Buddha manifests a body and awakens sentient beings." This principle is clarified in that from the morning of attaining the way until the evening of parinirvana, Buddha discoursed freely, without words getting in the way.

Buddha manifests a body and awakens sentient beings. There is no other activity for a Buddha but this. Every action of an awakened person is for the purpose of awakening sentient beings, but without necessarily any intention to do so. It is only the natural functioning of a Buddha: awakening beings. Manifesting a body from moment to moment is the living Buddha-dharma. The words expressed by a Buddha are not hindered by self; they flow freely and they are the very life of the Dharma. They are not words about the Dharma or spiritless explanations, but the living Truth. The Buddha taught freely from the moment of his enlightenment until his passing into *parinirvana*. It is precisely the same for all the great Patriarchs.

Notes

[1] From *Denkoroku*, unpublished translation by Koun Yamada and Robert Aitken.

Only Buddha and Buddha
Part Four

An ancient Buddha said:

The entire universe is the true human body.
The entire universe is the gate of liberation.
The entire universe is the eye of Vairochana.
The entire universe is the Dharma body of the self.

"The true human body" means your own true body. Know that the entire universe is your own true body, which is not a temporary body.

If someone asks you why we do not usually notice this, say, "Just reflect within yourself that the entire universe is the true human body." Or say, "The entire universe is the true human body—you already know this."

Also, "The entire universe is the gate of liberation" means that you are not at all entangled or captivated. What is called "the entire universe" is undivided from the moment, the ages, mind and words. This limitless and boundless experience is the "entire universe." Even if you seek to enter or go through this gate of libera-

tion, it cannot be done. How is this so? Reflect on the questions raised. If you intend to seek outside what is, nothing will be attained.

"The entire universe is the eye of Vairochana" means that Buddhas have a single eye. Do not suppose that a Buddha's eye is like those of human beings.

Human beings have two eyes, but when you say "a human eye," you don't say "two eyes" or "three eyes." Those who study the teaching should not understand that "the eye of a Buddha," "the eye of Dharma," or "the celestial eye" is like the two eyes of human beings. To believe that it is like human eyes is lamentable. Understand now that there is only a Buddha's single eye, which is itself the entire universe.

A Buddha may have one thousand eyes or myriad eyes. But presently it is said that the entire universe is the one eye of Vairochana. Therefore, it is not mistaken to say that this eye is one of many eyes of a Buddha, just as it is not mistaken to understand that a Buddha has only one eye. A Buddha indeed has many kinds of eyes—three eyes, one thousand eyes, or eighty-four thousand eyes. Do not be surprised to hear that there are eyes such as these.

Also learn that the entire universe is the Dharma body of the self. To seek to know the self is invariably the wish of living beings. However, those who see the true self are rare. Only Buddhas know the true self.

People outside the way regard what is not the self as the self. But what Buddhas call the self is the entire universe. Therefore, there is never an entire universe that is not the self, with or without our knowing it. On this matter defer to the words of the ancient Buddhas.

The entire universe is the true human body. It is the gate of liberation, the eye of Vairochana Buddha, and the Dharma body of self. The true body is the entire universe; they are not two, but are inseparable from the beginning.

This very body is the gate of liberation. There is no other gate other than this body. This is what is known as the gateless gate of Zen. Since there was never any delusion to begin with, there is no enlightenment to be attained. Only dualistic understanding creates the idea that there is a gate to go through and any liberation to be found. There is no other shore to be reached; this is already the other shore. Your very body is the body of Vairochana Buddha; your very eye, the eye of Vairochana Buddha. This very eye is the entire universe. This eye has absolutely nothing to do with your two eyes. But if you look for this eye apart from this very body, you will not find it. If you look between your eyebrows, you will not find it there either.

To realize the Way of the Buddhas-Patriarchs is to realize this very body is the body of the Buddha. Do not look for your true self apart from this very body and mind. To begin with, there is no true self and no false self. There is only one Self, which is no-self, the gate of liberation, the eye of Vairochana Buddha. You should know that the whole universe is your own true body, unborn and undying.

If you are truly accomplished in the Way, you should be able to manifest the unborn Buddha-mind. This mind is no other than the mind which cuts vegetables and sweeps the floor. If you seek this mind apart from cutting vegetables and sweeping the floor, it is like searching for another head to put on your shoulders. You must go beyond the sacred and the profane: seeing with the same eyes and hearing with the same ears as all the Buddhas-Patriarchs. Don't bind yourself without so much as a rope. Don't fetter yourself with golden chains. Only put your head through the iron yoke that has no hole and instantaneously manifest the body that awakens all sentient beings.

Why is it that ordinary sentient beings do not realize the truth that the entire universe is the true human body, the gate of liberation, the eye of Vairochana Buddha, the Dharma body of the self? It is only because ordinary people are caught by dualistic thinking and do not realize their own treasure. They should reflect within on Dogen Zenji's words, "The entire universe is the true human body." Since you already know this, there is no awakening and no liberation. It is only because ordinary people lack faith in the Way and cling desperately to their belief in good and evil, right and wrong, that they are unable to be completely free. Those who are willing to reflect within themselves that the entire universe is the true human body can surely awaken the Bodhi-mind and liberate all sentient beings.

"The entire universe is the gate of liberation" means that you are not entangled or captivated: since the whole world is undivided to begin with, there is no delusion, no entanglement, and no confusion. Bodhi-mind is limitless and boundless, with no beginning and no end. It is no other than this very body and mind which stands six feet tall. Don't think that this limitless and boundless mind is other than this very body. No matter how hard you work to go through the gate of liberation, you will never succeed.

It is like Daitsu Chisho Buddha, who sat in zazen for ten kalpas and could not attain Buddhahood. He did not become a Buddha. Why was this so? It is precisely because Daitsu Chisho Buddha is a non-attained Buddha. You are just like this. You can practice on your cushion for countless ages and you will never attain Buddhahood. Whatever it is that you attain will not be Buddhahood, but only a figment of your imagination.

Since you have never been deluded from the beginning, there is no need for you to wander here and there, searching for the true eye of Vairochana Buddha. The very eye that is no-eye is the true eye of Vairochana Buddha. The very body which is no-body is the true body of the entire universe. If you look to the outside for your true self, you will attain nothing; if you look within, you also will find nothing. It is only when you cease looking either inside or outside that the true self is revealed as the true Dharma body, awakening all sentient beings, manifesting as the body of the Buddha.

There is only a Buddha's single eye, which is itself the entire universe. The whole universe is no other than Buddha's one eye. Don't think for a moment that it has anything to do whatsoever with two, three, or more eyes of human beings.

It is not a mistake to understand that a Buddha has only one eye. It is also not a mistake to understand that a Buddha has two eyes. Some Buddhas have twenty-twenty vision, others are near-sighted, and some are even far-sighted. A Buddha indeed has many kinds of eyes—three eyes, one thousand eyes, eighty-four thousand eyes—these are all the eyes of the One Body. Nothing escapes the eighty-four thousand eyes of this Buddha!

Cause and effect cannot be ignored. If you don't understand this, you may go about slandering the Buddha and Patriarchs. Such action will surely cause suffering. Only deluded sentient beings ignore the law of causation. Not even an enlightened Buddha is free from karma, and yet an enlightened Buddha is not bound by karma. The enlightened person goes far beyond such notions, and, like Master Joshu, does not even know about such things, entering the heavens to save celestial beings, going down into the deepest hell to rescue the devils, with no regard for his own human body.

To realize that the entire universe is the Dharma body of the self is the wish of all living beings. Some are aware of this wish and others are unaware. Although this is the wish of all living beings, only a few awaken completely to the true self. Only Buddhas know this self. The deluded continue to seek for this self apart from their own human body, believing that this body is somehow insufficient and inadequate, lacking the wisdom and purity to be the entire universe, the gate of liberation, the body of Shakyamuni.

People outside the Way regard what is not the self as the self. They see a false self as themselves and therefore seek to find a true self, which is not themselves. This is an unfortunate state of affairs. It is only because they do not comprehend fully the profound wisdom of the Buddha Shakyamuni that they go on endlessly transmigrating through the three worlds. If they would only cut the root of delusion with a single stroke of Manjusri's sword, they would realize the True body.

What Buddhas call the self is no other than the entire universe as oneself. Buddhas make no separation between the entire universe and their own human body. Lacking nothing from the beginning, they seek after nothing, having gone far beyond any such notions as enlightened or deluded. The entire universe is no other than the self, whether or not you realize it. Some will realize this fact, others will not. Those who do not realize it are not necessarily bad people, only deluded. Those who do realize it are not necessarily good people, only Buddhas.

Only Buddha and Buddha
Part Five

---·--·--·--·--◈--·--·--·--·---

Long ago a monk asked an old master, "When hundreds,
thousands, or myriads of objects come all at once, what should be
done?"

The master replied, "Don't try to control them."

What he means is that in whatever way objects come, do not
try to change them. Whatever comes is the Buddha-dharma, not
objects at all. Do not understand the master's reply as merely a
brilliant admonition, but realize that it is the truth. Even if you try
to control what comes, it cannot be controlled.

Even if it is hundreds, thousands, or myriads of objects,
whatever appears is no other than the Buddha-dharma; they
are not objects at all. This is the Truth and should be realized
as such. Whatever appears, do not try to control it, for it cannot be controlled. Hold no preference for or against it, for all
such preferences only keep you stuck to the wheel of birth
and death. It is only due to the attachment to your likes and
dislikes, loves and aversions, that you go on transmigrating
through the three worlds.

Dogen Zenji points out very clearly what our basic problem is: we cannot allow things to be just as they are. We are always trying to control everything and everyone. As the ten thousand dharmas appear, just let them be. They will go of their own accord. Whatever appears is Buddha, not thing.

This is the very truth. Whatever you do, whatever you say, from morning until night is nothing but the Buddha-dharma in realization. That is all you need to understand.

All kinds of objects appear in the mind. How do you go beyond attachment to these objects? Just give up control. Don't try to get rid of what you dislike or cling to whatever you like. Most of all, do not think of anything as your enemy; such thoughts are the result of being entangled in something that in reality does not exist.

One of the first lessons that you learn from sitting is that you cannot suppress what arises. Life cannot be controlled, and yet we keep on trying. It always ends in disappointment and frustration. Even love can become an excuse to control others.

How do you understand not picking and choosing? If you understand it to mean that you cannot pick and choose, then you do not truly understand the more profound meaning of "hold no preferences." Only a deluded person would bind himself with such a notion. A liberated person, when it is necessary, just chooses. Don't be dualistic, for if you are, you may be unable even to go shopping when you need groceries. You might stand in front of the meat counter and not be able to tell the poor butcher what you prefer, steak or pork chops. You might not even be able to find your way home from the supermarket if you cannot make distinctions and have no preferences.

A monk asked Joshu, "You say, 'The supreme way is not difficult, it simply dislikes choosing.' Isn't that a pit into which people today have fallen?" Joshu said, "Once someone asked me about that. Since then, for five years, I haven't been able to apologize for it."[1]

Until you realize Buddha, you cannot even recognize Buddha, for your projections get in the way. Until you let go of all preconceived notions and beliefs, you cannot recognize Buddha and so cannot receive the transmission. Only Buddha can receive Buddha. Only Buddha can transmit to Buddha. Until you are Buddha, whatever you receive is not the true transmission. Unfortunately, this is not always properly understood.

A monk said to Joshu, "I have heard about the stone bridge of Joshu for a long time. But I've come and found just a simple log bridge." Joshu said, "You see only the simple log bridge, and you don't see the stone bridge." The monk asked, "What is the stone bridge?" Joshu said, "Donkeys or horses cross."[2]

The monk is expecting to find some great enlightened person. Instead, he sees only a simple old monk. Joshu is saying, "You see only a simple monk, but you do not recognize the great master." The monk is asking, "Where is the great master?" And Joshu tells him, "Even asses and horses, like yourself, can use me to cross over to the other shore!"

Master Engo says: "The sacred sword is ever in hand: it is death-dealing and life-giving. It is there, it is here, simultaneously giving and taking. If you want to hold fast, you are free to hold fast. If you want to let go, you are free to let go. Tell me how it will be when one makes no distinction between host and guest, and is indifferent to which role one takes up."[3]

A monk came to Ukyu from the assembly of Joshu Osho. Ukyu asked him, "What difference do you find between Joshu's Dharma path and ours?" The monk said, "No difference." Ukyu said, "If there is no difference, then go back there," giving him a blow with his stick. The monk said, "Your stick should have eyes on top. You should not strike me so wantonly." Ukyu said, "Here is a fellow who is good to beat today," and gave him three more blows. The monk went out. Ukyu called after him, and said, "I gave a blind stick, as there is a fellow who deserved it." The monk turned and said, "It can't be helped, as the stick is in the hand of Your Reverence." Ukyu said, "If you need this stick, I will let you have it." The monk came nearer and snatched the stick from Ukyu's hand and gave him three blows. Ukyu said, "Blind stick, blind stick." The monk said, "There is a fellow who deserved it." Ukyu said, "It is a pity to beat a fellow wantonly." The monk promptly made obeisance to him. Ukyu said, "You made a bow—it is right for you?" The monk laughed loudly, and went out. Ukyu said, "Right, right!"[4]

Ukyu is asking the monk, "What is the difference between great Master Joshu's teaching and mine?" The monk answers, "No difference." This monk would not even be able to recognize the difference between his pride and his joy. Ukyu then reprimands him, "If you can't see a difference, then what are you doing coming here? Go back to Joshu's place!" giving him the blow he deserves. Then the monk has the audacity to imply, "You are blind and can't discern my realization. You should not hit me like that!" Ukyu beats him again and says, "You deserve to be beaten, you dumb fellow!" The monk turns and says, "Such inappropriate treatment can't be helped since the stick is in the hands of such a poor teacher as you." Ukyu offers, "If you think you are better than I am, here, take the stick!" The monk, grabbing the stick, beats Ukyu and Ukyu shouts, "You blind idiot!" The monk then says, "You deserved the blows." Ukyu says, "It's a shame that you hit this old monk so irresponsibly." The monk immediately makes a bow. Ukyu asks him, "Is it right for you to make such a bow? Do you really see anything?" The monk laughs loudly and leaves. At this, Ukyu was pleased: "Very good! Very good!"

Notes

1 *Hekiganroku*, Case 58, unpublished translation by Koun Yamada and Robert Aitken.
2 *Hekiganroku*, Case 52, unpublished translation by Koun Yamada and Robert Aitken.
3 *Hekiganroku*, Case 75. Engo's Introduction, Sekida, 342.
4 *Hekiganroku*, Case 75, unpublished translation by Koun Yamada and Robert Aitken.

Only Buddha and Buddha
Part Six

*An ancient Buddha said, "The mountains, rivers, and earth
are born at the same moment with each person. All Buddhas of the
three worlds are practicing together with each person."*

*If we look at the mountains, rivers, and earth when a person
is born, his birth does not seem to be bringing forth additional
mountains, rivers, and earth on top of the existing ones. Yet the
ancient Buddha's word cannot be mistaken. How should we understand this? Even if you do not understand it, you should not ignore
it. So, be determined to understand it. Since this word is already
expounded, you should listen to it. Listen until you understand.*

*This is how to understand. Is there anyone who knows what
his birth in its beginning or end is like? No one knows either birth's
end or its beginning; nevertheless everyone is born. Similarly, no
one knows the extremities of the mountains, rivers, and earth, but
all see this place and walk here. Do not think with regret that the
mountains, rivers, and earth are not born with you. Understand
that the ancient Buddha teaches that your birth is nonseparate
from the mountains, rivers, and earth.*

*Again, all Buddhas of the three worlds have already prac-
ticed, attained the way, and completed realization. How should we
understand that those Buddhas are practicing together with us?
First of all, examine a Buddha's practice. A Buddha's practice is to
practice with all beings, it is not a Buddha's practice. This being so,
all Buddhas, from the moment of attaining realization, realize and
practice the Way together with the entire universe and all beings.*

*You may have doubts about this. But the ancient Buddha's
word was expounded in order to clarify your confused thinking. Do
not think that Buddhas are other than you. According to this teaching, when all Buddhas of the three worlds arouse the thought of
enlightenment and practice, they never exclude our body-and-
mind. You should understand this. To doubt this is to slander the
Buddhas of the three worlds.*

*When we reflect quietly, it appears that our body-and-mind
has practiced together with all Buddhas of the three worlds and has
together with them aroused the thought of enlightenment. When we
reflect on the past and future of our body-and-mind, we cannot
find the boundary of self or others. By what delusion do we believe
our body-and-mind is apart from all Buddhas of the three worlds?
Such delusion is groundless. How then can delusion hinder the
arousing of the thought of enlightenment and the practicing of the
Way by all Buddhas of the three worlds? Thus, understand that the
Way is not a matter of your knowing or not knowing.*

Mountains, rivers, and the great earth are born simultaneously with you at the moment of your birth. This comes
directly out of realization and does not mean that mountains,
rivers, and the earth are created in duplicate each time someone is born. It would be completely wrong to understand the
statement in this way. You are not separate from the moun-

tains, rivers, and great earth, and should penetrate to the very heart of this teaching.

When you look into yourself, you find no beginning and no end, only this very life, without birth and without death. No one can find either birth's beginning or its end; nonetheless you are born and you die. This very body-mind is the unborn Buddha-mind. Even though you walk on the earth and appreciate the mountains and rivers, you cannot fathom the full extent of mountains, rivers, and the great earth. It is like trying to comprehend the enormity of the Grand Canyon. It cannot be grasped. Only no-mind can embrace it. All the great Buddha-Patriarchs taught that your life is not separate from the entire universe.

It is all One; this is the realization. As Shakyamuni Buddha put it when he attained enlightenment, "I and all sentient beings and the great earth have in the same moment attained the Way!" As soon as the slightest distinction between self and others is made, then you create heaven and hell. When you let go, no distinctions appear and you realize that you are not two.

All Buddhas have already practiced, realized, and attained the Way. You should appreciate this, because all Buddhas of the three worlds are no other than you. For this reason, there is nothing to attain and no delusion to get rid of. When body and mind drop off, you understand the profundity of this statement. A Buddha does not practice by separating from all beings. The practice of all sentient beings is no other than the life of all Buddhas. When an ordinary sentient being awakens Bodhi-mind, from that very moment on, practice-realization is one with the entire universe and all beings.

This was Buddha's experience under the bodhi tree, and this must be realized by each of us. Without this profound realization, you will continue on the karmic wheel of endless suffering. This is the point of Zen practice, and Dogen Zenji is encouraging us each to awaken to this Truth.

Do not ever become satisfied. It is easy to be complacent and not continue to clarify the Way, which is to clarify the Self. It is an endless process. There is no one who can realize the full extent of mountains, rivers, and the great earth. It is seamless and whole. This is Buddha's enlightenment.

Since you may have doubts about this, all of Buddha's teaching is just to clarify your confusion. Do not be so deluded as to think that Buddhas are other than you! When all Buddhas awaken, what naturally arises is Bodhi-mind, the desire to liberate all sentient beings. This liberation is done with the whole body and mind. No Buddha has ever excluded body and mind when awakening sentient beings. You should understand this well. To doubt this is to slander all the Buddhas and Bodhisattvas of the three worlds.

When we reflect quietly, it appears that our body-and-mind has practiced together with all Buddhas of the three worlds and has together with them aroused the thought of enlightenment. When we reflect on the past and future of our body-and-mind, we cannot find the boundary of self or others. By what delusion do we believe our body-and-mind is apart from all Buddhas of the three worlds? Such delusion is groundless. How then can delusion hinder the arousing of the thought of enlightenment and the practicing of the Way by all Buddhas of the three worlds? Thus, understand that the Way is not a matter of your knowing or not knowing.

Through zazen you realize that body and mind are not

separate from all the Buddhas in the Ten Directions. When you awaken Bodhi-mind, you realize this is the same awakening as all the Buddhas throughout space and time. This is the essence of Buddha-dharma. All beings can awaken to the Bodhi-mind, as all past Buddhas have done.

When you turn your own light inward, you cannot find any beginning or any end to this Mind. Although it is constantly manifesting each moment, you cannot grasp it. Although you cannot grasp it, you are not far from it. If you are still seeking after it, you are mountains and rivers away from it.

The awakened Mind does not create a boundary between self and others. It is only deluded people who create boundaries and believe the self to be separate from all the Buddhas. Such delusion is groundless. When one is awakened, delusion cannot hinder the raising of the Bodhi-mind, practice, and realization. The Way has nothing to do with your knowing or not knowing. Knowing is delusion; not knowing is mere blankness. You must go beyond knowing and not knowing. Buddha-mind is beyond comprehension. It is completely ungraspable. That there is nothing which can be attained is not idle talk; it is the Truth.

Joshu once asked Nansen, "What is the Way?" Nansen answered, "Ordinary mind is the Way." "Then should we direct ourselves toward it or not?" asked Joshu. "If you try to direct yourself toward it, you go away from it," answered Nansen. Joshu continued, "If we do not try, how can we know that it is the Way?" Nansen replied, "The Way does not belong to knowing or to not-knowing. Knowing is illusion; not-knowing is blankness. If you really attain to the Way of no-doubt, it is like the great void, so vast and boundless. How, then, can there be right and wrong in the Way?" At these words, Joshu was suddenly enlightened.

Mumon's commentary: "Questioned by Joshu, Nansen immediately shows that the tile is disintegrating, the ice is dissolving, and no communication whatsoever is possible. Even though Joshu may be enlightened, he can truly get it only after studying for thirty more years."[1]

Notes

[1] *Mumonkan*, Case 19, Shibayama, 140.

Only Buddha and Buddha
Part Seven

A teacher of old said, "Chopping down is nothing other than chopping down; moving about is beyond discussion. Mountains, rivers, and earth are the entirely revealed body of the Dharma king.

A person of the present should study this phrase of the teacher of old. There is a Dharma king who understands that the body of the Dharma king is not different from chopping down, just as mountains are on earth, and the earth is holding up mountains.

When you understand, a moment of no-understanding does not come and hinder understanding, and understanding does not break no-understanding. Instead, understanding and no-understanding are just like spring and autumn.

However, when you do not understand, the pervasive voice of Dharma does not reach your ears; in the midst of the voice your ears dally about. But when you understand, the voice has already reached your ears; samadhi has emerged.

Know that no-understanding cannot be discerned by a self; the Dharma king's understanding is just like this.

In the Dharma king's body the eye is just like the body, and the mind is the same as the body. There is not the slightest gap between mind and body; everything is fully revealed. Similarly, you should understand that in illumination and discourse the Dharma king's body is revealed.

Mountains and rivers, the great earth, are all Buddha. Everything that appears is the manifestation of the unborn Buddha-mind. This is a fact whether the mountains and rivers are aware of it or not. Each thing is Buddha and everyone is Buddha. Some will become aware of this Truth and others will not.

You should first clarify the question: who is the Dharma king? Is the Dharma king some mystical character? Where was he born? Who were his parents? Is he tall or short? Fat or thin? The Dharma king is no other than Buddha Shakyamuni. Buddha Shakyamuni is no other than you. You and the Dharma king are not two.

How do you understand that your body and the body of the Dharma king are not different from "chopping down"? All your activity from morning until night is no other than the manifestation of Dharma king, just as the earth contains the mountains and the mountains rest on the earth. You rest within the Dharma king and the Dharma king rests within you.

The discriminating mind cannot hinder or dilute Bodhi-mind. This Mind can never be touched or destroyed, even if you are going through all kinds of difficulties. When you are completely identified with this unborn Buddha-mind, you are the Master. No one can hurt you. Having complete faith, you are fearless. Even death and the prospect of going to hell are no more frightening than taking a walk in the park on a Sunday afternoon.

How do you understand "a moment of no-understanding"? Do you expect that "you" will realize anything when you attain realization? Realization attains realization itself. "You" are not to be found. The experience of enlightenment is beyond experience and no-experience. It is a nonexperience. Nonunderstanding does not in any way hinder true understanding, nor does understanding disrupt nonunderstanding. They are like the spring and autumn, or like the foot before and the foot behind in walking; one just follows the other without any problem. Both are the manifestation of the Dharma king. You should clarify these words.

All things that drop down before man are the Dharma king in realization. All things coexist within the One, even without being aware of this mutual interpenetration. Buddhas and sentient beings coexist without affecting one another. The only difference is that sentient beings believe there to be a difference, while Buddhas know there is no difference. Those who are not open and receptive will gain absolutely nothing from these words. One might just as well be whistling in the wind. Those who are ready for this teaching will awaken to their true nature and be one with all dharmas. Those who do not awaken should not blame the ancient masters, but should seek out a true teacher and study with all earnestness. It is only through your own determination and effort under the guidance of a living master that you will clarify the Way and attain to the Dharma king.

Emperor Shukuso asked Chu Kokushi, "What is the ten-bodied herdsman?" Chu Kokushi said, "Go trampling on Vairochana's head!" The emperor said, "I cannot follow you."

Chu Kokushi said, "Don't take the self for the pure Dharma body."[1]

If you have even the slightest dualistic thought, then you are completely deluded. If you think that you and the Dharma body are two, you cannot even save yourself from endless transmigration. How do you understand this? If you cannot answer, the Zen school shall surely perish.

Master Engo had this to say: "When the dragon calls, mists and clouds arise; when the tiger roars, gales begin to blow. The supreme teachings of the Buddha ring out with a silvery voice. The actions of Zen masters are like those of the most expert archers, whose arrows, shot from opposite directions, collide in midair. The truth is revealed for all ages and all places. Tell me, who has ever been like this?"[2]

Know that no-understanding cannot be discerned by a self; the Dharma king's understanding is just like this.

In the Dharma king's body the eye is just like the body, and the mind is the same as the body. There is not the slightest gap between mind and body; everything is fully revealed. Similarly, you should understand that in illumination and discourse the Dharma king's body is revealed.

It is only through the great benevolent compassion of the Dharma king that you shall awaken. Being awakened has nothing to do with awareness. Trees and mountains are already Buddhas; they don't need to become aware of it. So what are you waiting for? Are you waiting to become aware of something? Just drop all your preconceptions and carry on with your life. You lack nothing from the beginning. The only barrier is your idea of what "it" should be. You cannot even begin to conceive of "it," so why don't you just be your ordinary self with nothing further to seek after. Carry your bundles and sweep out your garage. Isn't it long overdue?

Notes

[1] *Hekiganroku*, Case 99, Main Case, Sekida, 398.
[2] *Hekiganroku*, Case 99, Master Engo's Introduction, Sekida, 398.

Only Buddha and Buddha
Part Eight

—·—·—·—·—·—◆—·—·—·—·—·—

There has been a saying since olden times: "No one except a fish knows a fish's heart, no one except a bird follows a bird's trace."

Yet those who really understand this principle are rare. To think that no one knows a fish's heart or a bird's trace is mistaken. You should know that fish always know one another's heart, unlike people who do not know one another's heart. But when the fish try to go up through the Dragon Gate, they know one another's intention and have the same heart. Or they share the heart of breaking through the Nine Great Bends. Those who are not fish hardly know this.[1]

Only a Buddha can know a Buddha. Just as only a fish knows the heart of a fish and only a bird follows a bird's trace, no one but a Buddha can discern the heart of a Buddha. Only a Buddha can transmit to a Buddha, as only a Buddha can receive from a Buddha. Ordinary people cannot know the heart of a Buddha, just as humans cannot know the hearts of either fish or birds. If you want to be completely free and at peace, you must fully clarify this point. A Buddha cannot transmit the Dharma to an ordinary person, just as an ordinary person is not ready to receive the transmission from a Buddha. Until you have realized your own unborn Buddha-mind and the Buddha-mind of all ancestors, you will not be an empty vessel. Few really understand this principle. Those who do are indeed rare.

Only fish can know the heart of fish, and only birds can know their path of migration. If you have profound understanding, you will realize that fish are aware of each other's hearts and in this respect are different from ordinary people. There is a unity of heart when fish swim against a strong current or negotiate a swift, meandering river. Fish and birds are in such harmony, for they are truly one mind. It is just like this for Buddhas, but not for ordinary people. Buddhas live in harmony and their heart is one, whereas ordinary people live in conflict and chaos.

In a Zen monastery everything is done together. When it is time to sit, everybody sits; and when it is time to eat, everybody eats. This can bring up a lot of resistance, especially for Westerners, who are prone to stress their individuality. But anyone who has undergone Zen training for some time will begin to sense a subtle communication with others. Under the right circumstances and the guidance of a teacher, a group of practitioners can learn to function as one body-mind. It is not easy to find an opportunity to train the way Dogen Zenji recommends, but in order to practice as he instructs and to experience the teaching of the true Dharma, it is essential to undergo such training.

When you surrender your personal self to the practice, then your life manifests the Buddha-dharma; the Buddha-dharma functions freely and without restraint, because your life is the life of everyone and everything. When you retain your personal self, then your life is not manifested as the Buddha-dharma, but as your personal life.

Practice is ordinary life and nothing special; but ordinary life is not always practice, because the Buddha Way is the Supreme Way. That is the reason, according to Zen Master Dogen, that the gateway to practice-realization is leaving home and abandoning personal life. When there is no personal life, practice is boundless and countless Buddhas and Tathagatas come together.

Keizan Zenji said: "The source of mind is oceanically calm and the sea of Dharma is fathomless; one who cannot realize it will wander eternally and one who realizes it will be immediately at home. To be able to play freely in the field of enlightenment, it is necessary to cut the root of human attachment. Because it is one with the Way of all Enlightened Ones, to abide in nonabiding is instantaneous enlightenment. Do not doubt this!"[2]

Nothing surpasses relinquishment of self for allowing both mind and body to become one with the Buddha Way. When one drops off body and mind, one's true body is immediately revealed as the body of the Buddha. Stepping outside worldly delusion is to realize freedom of functioning. Those who have relinquished the self feel a sense of gratitude to the Buddhas and Patriarchs that is deeper than the sea and higher than the mountains. When even this sense of gratitude is transcended, they enter a state of eternal purity. Their lives are freely devoted to the welfare and service of all beings.

Again, when a bird flies in the sky, beasts do not even dream of finding or following its trace. As they do not know that there is such a thing, they cannot even imagine this. However, a bird can see traces of hundreds and thousands of small birds having passed in flocks, or traces of so many lines of large birds having flown south or north. Those traces may be even more evident than the carriage tracks left on a road or the hoofprints of a horse seen in the grass. In this way, a bird sees birds' traces.

Buddhas are like this. You may wonder how many lifetimes Buddhas have been practicing. Buddhas, large or small, although they are countless, all know their own traces. You never know a Buddha's trace when you are not a Buddha.

Since birds in flight leave no visible trace, they are impossible for animals and people on the ground to track. Another bird, however, can see their traces and follow them. For birds, the traces of its predecessors are clearer than the muddy tracks of a carriage or the hoofprints of a horse in the grass. A bird does not need such marks in order to follow the path of its predecessors.

It is just like this for Buddhas. Only a Buddha can follow the path of all his ancestors, because it is only a Buddha who is intimate with the One Mind of all the Buddhas. Only a Buddha has the Buddha-eye, and without this eye the Supreme Way cannot be seen. Therefore it is only a Buddha who can understand and know the teachings of all the past Buddhas. It is only a Buddha who practices as a Buddha. Sentient beings practice as ordinary people with ordinary clothes. Buddhas wear Buddha's robe and eat Buddha's food out of Buddha's bowls.

Those who are unable to appreciate Buddha's Supreme Vehicle because they cannot see the traces of all the past Buddhas often search for more clear and obvious tracks. These tracks usually come in the form of words and letters. They follow the written teachings and the rules and regulations of the Buddha instead. This is perfectly acceptable, for everyone has his or her own karma, but it is not the heart of the Buddha. Only a Buddha knows the heart of all the Buddhas, and only a Buddha can see the traces of all the past Buddhas. If you practice Zen, but have not yet had the good fortune to become one with the Buddha-mind, you may be tempted to keep groping for clear outward expressions—such as characteristic signs of a Buddha, or standards and codes of behavior—as well-defined as the tracks of a carriage in the mud.

A monk asked Master Obaku, "Does the Buddha really liberate sentient beings?" Master Obaku answered, "There are in reality no sentient beings to be delivered by the Tathagata. If even self has no objective existence, how much less has other-than-self! Thus, neither Buddha nor sentient beings exist objectively."

The Monk continued, "Yet it is recorded that 'Whosoever possesses the thirty-two characteristic signs of a Buddha is able to deliver sentient beings.' How can you deny it?" Obaku answered, "Anything possessing any signs is illusory. It is by perceiving that all signs are no signs that you perceive the Tathagata. Buddha and sentient beings are both your own false conceptions. It is because you do not know real Mind that you delude yourselves with such objective concepts. If you will conceive of a Buddha, you will be obstructed by that Buddha! And when you conceive of sentient beings, you will be obstructed by those beings. All such dualistic concepts as ignorant and enlightened, pure and impure, are obstructions. It is because your minds are hindered by them that the Wheel of the Dharma must be turned.

Just as apes spend their time throwing feces away and picking them up again unceasingly, so it is with you and your learning. All you need is to give up your learning, your ignorant and enlightened, pure and impure, great and little, your attachment and activity. Such things are mere conveniences, mere ornaments within the One Mind. I hear you have studied the sutras of the twelve divisions of the Three Vehicles. They are all mere empirical concepts. Really you must give them up!

"So just discard all you have acquired as being no better than a bedspread for you when you were sick. Only when you have abandoned all perceptions, there being nothing objective to perceive; only when phenomena obstruct you no longer; only when you have rid yourself of the whole gamut of dualistic concepts of the ignorant and enlightened category, will you at last earn the title of Transcendental Buddha. Therefore it is written: 'Your prostrations are in vain. Put no faith in such ceremonies. Hie from such false beliefs.' Since Mind knows no divisions into separate entities, phenomena must be equally undifferentiated. Since Mind is above all activities, so must it be with phenomena. Every phenomenon that exists is a creation of thought; therefore I need but empty my mind to discover that all of them are void. It is the same with all sense-objects to whichever of the myriads of categories they belong. The entire void stretching out in all directions is of one substance with Mind; and, since Mind is fundamentally undifferentiated, so must it be with everything else. Different entities appear to you only because your perceptions differ—just as the colors of the precious delicacies eaten by the Devas are said to differ in accordance with the individual merits of the Devas eating them.

"*Anuttara-samyak-sambodhi* is a name for the realization that the Buddhas of the whole universe do not in fact possess the smallest perceptible attribute. There exists just the One Mind. Truly there are no multiplicity of forms, no Celestial Brilliance, and no Glorious Victory (over *samsara*) or submission to the Victor. Since no Glorious Victory was ever won, there can be no such formal entity as a Buddha; and, since no submission ever took place, there can be no such formal entities as sentient beings."[3]

You may wonder why you do not know. The reason is that, while Buddhas see these traces with a Buddha's eye, those who are not Buddhas do not have a Buddha's eye, and just notice the Buddha's attributes.

All who do not know should search out the trace of the Buddha's path. If you find footprints, you should investigate whether they are the Buddha's. On being investigated, the Buddha's trace is known; and whether it is long or short, shallow or deep, is also known. To illuminate your trace is accomplished by studying the Buddha's trace. Accomplishing this is Buddha-dharma.

You should ask yourself why you cannot follow and know Buddha's Supreme Teaching. It is clear that while Buddhas can follow the path of all the Buddha-Patriarchs, those who are not yet enlightened do not have the eye of a Buddha, so they search for attributes and characteristics that fit their preconceived idea of what a Buddha should look like. These people would not even be able to recognize a Buddha if he sat down in their midst. They would be busy looking for the characteristerics and qualities that they have dreamt up.

Seeing only their own projections of good and evil, they would miss the old barbarian even if he hit them over the head.

To illuminate your trace is accomplished by studying the Buddha's trace. You can only know the Buddha's trace if you forget yourself, give up all notions, and relinquish everything. It seems completely irresponsible, but it is not. Those who have this idea don't know the true liberation of clinging to absolutely nothing. Because they never experienced the complete liberation of relinquishment, they are afraid to even watch others go through that process. Drifting and wandering through the Three Worlds, it is very difficult to cut off human attachment and ties; and yet it is impossible to receive the whole teaching if you try to hold onto anything, whether it be your ideas, your home, your job, or your loved ones.

For Zen students it is of the utmost importance that they are allowed the opportunity by their teacher to give up their life. This is an expression of true gratitude. To hold on to conventional sanity is madness. To let go of sanity is to go beyond sanity and madness.

Notes

1 Dragon gate: rapids midway up the Huong River, where fish who pass are said to turn into dragons. Nine Great Bends: the Huong River is said to have nine major bends along its course.

2 Adapted from Keizan Zenji, *Raisanmon*, unpublished translation by Maezumi Roshi.

3 Huang Po, 70–72.

菩提薩埵四攝法

Bodaisatta Shishobo

The Four Benevolent Ways of the Bodhisattva

The four ways a Bodhisattva acts to benefit human beings are: fuse (dana), *giving or generosity;* aigo, *loving or compassionate speech;* rigyo, *beneficial action; and* doji, *identification with others.*

The Four Benevolent Ways of the Bodhisattva
Generosity

———————◈———————

Fuse *also means* futon, *which is not to covet or be greedy;
not to flatter, adulate, nor curry favor. Even a king who controls the
whole world must have* futon *if he wishes to propagate the right
way. Only by the virtue of* futon *can he build a peaceful world. The
virtue of* futon *is like the virtue you grant to jewels and to people
that you do not know: without greed or malice. It is the same as
offering a flower that blooms in the far mountains to a Buddha, or
offering precious jewels or a previous life to a sentient being. We
possess in our original nature the virtue of generosity, spiritual or
material, in each moment. Although in principle nothing belongs to
self, you can be generous. It is of no concern whether the gift is
large or small: the important point is whether it can be beneficial to
others. The merit of generosity itself bears fruit. If you entrust and
commit yourself to the Way, you will be complete. In such ways
treasure begets treasure, and becomes generosity. You give generously yourself and accordingly others too give generously. The motivating power of giving pierces heavenly beings, human beings,*

saints and sages, and leads to complete enlightenment. This is due to innen *(causal motivation) for generous actions.*

Only by being truly generous is the Buddha Way manifested. Giving is the most direct path to liberation. All sentient beings attain enlightenment simultaneously with complete relinquishment of self.

A peaceful world can only be accomplished when people have awakened Bodhi-mind. As long as there is self-clinging and greed, the world remains in delusion and confusion. Original nature possesses infinite capacity to give, materially and spiritually, in each moment. Although nothing belongs to self to begin with, you can give endlessly just by cutting off the root of dualistic thinking, which separates self and others. Although you do not possess anything you can still give. That is the miracle. As long as you trust in the Dharma, you will never run short. It is of no concern whether the gift is large or small, only whether it benefits others or not. The very act of giving itself bears fruit. If you give yourself to the Buddha Way wholeheartedly, your life will be complete and fulfilled. In such a way your own Buddha treasure is revealed and becomes generosity.

Although everyone gives, true generosity is rare. Even while giving, we often act out of self-interest. Ego has a difficult time being generous. The coveting mind expects something in return and thinks it knows what is best for others. Instead of just giving generously what people are asking for, the petty mind would rather give what it believes they should have.

In a previous life, Shakyamuni Buddha came upon a lioness whose cubs were dying because she was starving and didn't have milk enough to feed them. He offered his own body as food. Laying himself down, he said, "Please eat me!" and she did. Suddenly the lioness turned into Kanzeon, Avalokitesvara Bodhisattva, who predicted that for this deed he would be reborn as Shakyamuni Buddha in the next lifetime and would become a great Bodhisattva. Only through generosity, complete relinquishment of the self, can you realize and actualize the Buddha Way. If you are compassionate and loving, then this illuminates the whole world; but practice alone is not enough to manifest true compassion. Compassion is the functioning of *prajna* wisdom.

When you give generously, you receive everything in return. Those to whom you are giving are no other than you. Those from whom you receive are also no other than you. No matter how it may appear to the discriminating mind, you are receiving and giving continuously. By allowing others to give, you are a Bodhisattva; by giving to others, you are also a Bodhisattva. If you can't receive, it means that you don't really know how to give, either. When you give with your whole heart, others are inspired to give likewise. When you give your whole life to the Buddha-dharma, others are inspired to do the same; if you don't, they are not. Giving your life to the Dharma doesn't make you a good person, only a Buddha. Those who do not give their lives to the Dharma are not bad, only ordinary.

Bodhi-mind, manifesting as generosity, motivates beings to give up the self and to accomplish the Buddha Way. This motivating power pierces heavenly beings, human beings, saints and sages, and leads to complete enlightenment. This is due to the karma and power of true giving.

Giving is enlightenment, and enlightenment is expressed by generosity. By giving yourself completely to all things, you are a Buddha. To give everything away is to be awakened by all things. All barriers drop, and you are one with the Buddha-dharma. It is simply the law of cause and effect. When you truly give, you give yourself away. When you truly realize Bodhi-mind, you stop the ceaselessly seeking mind. This gives you the time and space to be compassionate and generous.

Master Rinzai said: "Venerable ones, why are you running about desperately seeking everywhere, getting fallen arches from your ceaseless wanderings? There is no Buddha to seek, no Way to accomplish, no Dharma to be obtained. If you seek Buddha in external forms, he would not be more than yourself. Do you want to know your original heart? You can neither know it nor separate yourself from it. Followers of the Way, the true Buddha has no shape, the true Way has no substance, the true Dharma has no form. These three blend together harmoniously and unite into one. Who does not yet discern this is called a sentient being confused by karma."[1]

The Buddha said that when a donor comes to an assembly of monks, they will look respectfully at him. The meaning of this is that you do not look at the mind of the person who gives. One can touch the mind without words so you should be generous. One could give a single word or a verse of teaching to people, a small coin, or even a blade of grass. Such generosity can cause good deeds in this world and the next. The Dharma is a treasure, and treasure is the Dharma. This is due to the compassion of Bodhisattvas.

Just by being generous, you can touch people. By a single word or verse of teaching, the heart of others can be opened. Similarly if you give money, food, or other material things, people will appreciate your generosity. Such donations, when given freely and without expectations, sow the seeds of good karma in this life and future lives. The greatest gift possible is the opportunity to practice. Your life is the Dharma treasure, and the Dharma treasure is your very own life. This is due to the compassion of all the Buddhas and Bodhisattvas.

It is because only a Buddha can recognize a Buddha that so many people ignore this precious treasure. Looking for certain marks and characteristics, they miss the real Buddha. Some are fortunate enough to come in contact with the living Dharma, but still do not seize the opportunity to practice. Allowing one's convictions or society's standards to get in the way is no less than tragic. However reasonable it may seem to let the norm of the majority determine the behavior of individuals, awakened people do not always fit into this concept. In fact, it is impossible to drop the self and attain liberation by adhering to the norm; the norm is established and maintained to protect the self.

The very fact that we are all Buddha is equality at its most basic level, but this does not mean that everybody is the same. Within equality we are all uniquely different. As Dogen Zenji states in the "Genjokoan," "When all dharmas are realized as the Buddha-dharma, there are enlightenment and delusion, practice, life and death, Buddhas and ordinary people."[2] Even this first level of enlightenment is difficult to attain, but without realizing it at least to some degree, it is impossible to grow and to give in to something more vast than oneself.

Those who came upon practice early may not realize how fortunate they are. Many others wander for years, blind and aimless, before they encounter the true Dharma. There was a Catholic nun who was eighty-two when she came to practice. She broke down in tears and said, "I have been seeking for more than sixty years. I am crying in great gratitude, finally to have found the posture of zazen." Can you imagine, all those years of devotion and effort, only to find out that such a simple thing as sitting in the correct posture was all that was missing to allow her heart to open!

The priceless treasure of practice is due to the compassion of the Buddha and Bodhisattvas. Who are all these Bodhisattvas? They are none other than you and me! Master Rinzai realized it: "Nowadays I don't feel any different from the Buddha and the Patriarchs, from all the Bodhisattvas." Wasn't he an arrogant fellow?

The point is to realize that you are no other than the Buddha and all the Bodhisattvas. Just give yourself completely away. When you give everything up to the Dharma, the Dharma will take care of you. Just rest in this fact. The only thing lacking is faith in the Way. There is nothing further to attain. Only let go of yourself.

The following is an example of this:
There once was a king who tried to cure a sick minister by giving him medicine and burning his own beard. The people of his country trusted him. Also there was a child who, playing in a sand box, offered sand as food to the Buddha. Later, due to the merit of the action, the king ascended to the throne, for in both cases they both did what they could without expecting results.

Supplying a boat on the river or building a bridge are deeds of generosity. If you learn the real meaning of giving, you will know that to have a position in society and to act on behalf of society is also generosity. Politics and industry are themselves forms of giving. It is their nature just as when the time comes, the wind will cause a flower to drop, and the bird will chirp in accord with the seasons.

The key point here is doing or giving whatever possible without expecting anything in return. Materially you may not be able to give much; yet it is not what or how much you give but your attitude behind the giving which is essential. Give freely whatever you can without expecting a reward. You never owned any of it in the first place. It is impossible to have something completely for yourself. There simply is no one to do the possessing and nothing to be possessed. Everything is impermanent—empty and unsubstantial—and everyone is without self.

There are four major causes of suffering that arise from ignoring this Truth. The first one is that you can't have what you want. You may desire money, love, recognition, or enlightenment, yet nothing is satisfactory for very long, so there is always the craving for more. The more you get, the more you want. Then there is the opposite problem: you have something that you don't want and you would like to get rid of it—leg pain or an illness, or an unhappy relationship. Having what you don't want and wanting what you don't have, you fall victim to endless frustration. The third cause of suffering is loving someone and not being able to be close to that person; and the fourth is the opposite, having to be with someone you don't want to be with.

All of these four causes of suffering come down to one thing: not being able to accept things the way they are. Wanting more or wanting less, we always want things to be other than the way they are. Zazen is learning to stop separating ourselves from our environment and to be completely one with it.

When you learn the true meaning of generosity, you will understand that whatever your position in society you always have the opportunity to give. Whether you are a teacher, lawyer, carpenter, etc., you can give of yourself. Most people think that they have to attain something special or do something in particular before they can contribute and make a difference in the world. You lack nothing from the beginning and therefore are able to give freely. As long as you have the intention to give, there are endless opportunities to do so.

When you give yourself completely, there is no carry-over from one activity to another and you do not get distracted. You are completely one with the moment and therefore no traces are left. Yet it is difficult to do this. The best way to learn to give yourself fully to the task at hand is zazen. In zazen you learn to focus your attention and devote your whole body and mind to single-minded sitting. Then nothing remains of yourself; there is just giving without expectations, because there is no self involved.

Usually we want to be personally involved and assume that other people are similarly involved. If a boat is about to run into you while you are sailing on a river, you will probably get angry, thinking there is some fool at the rudder. The moment you notice that the boat is empty, just drifting with nobody in it, everything changes. The anger drops and you take care of the situation. Our practice is to see that there is no fixed self anywhere, not here in your boat nor there in the other person's boat.

As long as you see your teacher as a teacher, you don't mind being used as a vehicle for the Dharma, but when you want something personal from him or her, you will probably end up disappointed. Then you wonder why it is so difficult to accomplish the Way, and why you have so much trouble with the teacher.

Why is it so hard to be intimate? The conventional understanding of intimacy is two people relating personally to each other, treating each other as special people. Zen intimacy requires the vessels to be empty; then there is no relationship. The two are one, one empty self, one Mind. That is the true intimacy; it is communion.

If there is truly no self, then there is only what is in any given moment. The no-mind is the true Mind. There is only the situation, no separate self in relationship to it. When you are really at one with the situation, there is no fixed self; it is constantly shifting and changing. When you lose that kind of mobility and fluidity you get stuck, and immediately the situation becomes problematic.

Letting go, dropping off body and mind, has to happen continuously. That is *shikantaza*, that is enlightenment, being completely one with each situation, without any gap. Just as the birds sing in accord with the seasons, you respond according to what's going on. When it is hot you take off your jacket, when it is cool you just put it on again. When you are despised you are just being despised, when you are loved you are just being loved. With no separation from the ever-changing moment, everything is just as it is.

Great King Asoka, who was deeply devoted to Buddhism and who did not, until just before his death at a great age, lose his power, offered a half a mango to an assembly of monks. It was only a small mango, but it gave the assembly great merit.

People who wish to be generous should clarify this principle and make an effort not to lose any opportunity to give generously. You indeed in your original nature possess the merit to give generously, and although each person may be different, each has the opportunity to practice generosity.

The Buddha said you should take generosity as your own; moreover, you should give it to your parents, your wives, and children. Even if you use it as your own, it will still be generosity and what your parents, wives, husbands, and children will gain will also be generosity. Even if you only possess a mere trace of generosity, you will have joy in your hearts, for it becomes that which you correctly transmit to others, and this is done as a merit and a facet of the Buddha. Moreover, it is worthwhile even to practice one of the actions of a Bodhisattva.

You cannot change the minds of others, but if you give material gifts, you have a chance to show your mind of the Buddha Way and so can help it to change and experience the Way of enlightenment. To do this, you should certainly take a first step by beginning to practice generosity. In this way, generosity comes first among the six paramitas of the Bodhisattva. You cannot measure the size, great or small, of the mind, nor indeed can you measure the size of materials. There is, however, a time when mind changes materials and materials change mind. This is when both of them have generosity.

A few flowers or a smile, a gesture or a friendly word can bring great joy, but the greatest gift that can possibly be given is the gift of no-fear. To be free from fear means to awaken from the dream, from the illusion of a separate self. People who are asleep are not bad people; they are only dreaming. When they wake up, they are not particularly good, only awake. Realizing Bodhi-mind does not make one a particularly good person, only a Buddha. Somebody who remains deluded is not necessarily bad, only an ordinary person.

The point is to go beyond any dualistic understanding of good and bad, sanity or madness, and realize basic sanity. For a Buddha, the most important matter is not to encourage people to conform to society's norms, but to awaken sentient beings from delusion. An awakened person's compassion could even appear mad because it is beyond conventional understanding. There are countless examples in the history of Buddhism, especially in the Zen and Tibetan traditions.

While on pilgrimage, Monk Taigen did further study with Zen Master Gyo-o. When Taigen was about to depart, Master Gyo-o said, "Since I have nothing to give you, I should like to make this as my gift." Suddenly he picked up a red-hot charcoal from the hearth with the fire tongs and gave it to Taigen. Monk Taigen did not know how to receive it. He stomped out of the room and locked himself away for seven days. When he went to see Master Gyo-o again to say good-bye, Gyo-o did the same thing again. This time, however, Taigen had no hesitation in taking care of the matter, and the Master approved it.

The basic intention of enlightened people is to awaken others and give them the gift of no-fear; this is most precious and takes precedence over any other gift. There are no rules in this kind of giving. As in love and war, anything goes. Although a student may want to know how this gift is going to be given and have a say in how and when it is to be received, preparing for it kills the whole thing. It has to be sudden and unexpected. If you plan it ahead of time, it never works. The gift must arrive spontaneously out of no-self. Maybe that is why you have the best chance of getting enlightened by something completely unexpected, like a stone hitting a bamboo pole, the sudden striking of thunder, or the blow of the master's stick. Then no preparation is possible. In that instant of surprise, you become one, dropping off body and mind.

Seikenko of Cho composed this verse upon attaining enlightenment:

> Sitting in the room in absolute silence;
> Mind-source unmoved, filled like still water.
> The striking of thunder has opened the gate of
>   head's crown.
> The beginningless self-nature has been awakened.[3]

Those who devote themselves to the Buddha Way and give with their whole heart surely will attain the power to go beyond enlightenment and delusion. Such generosity is often blocked by the fear that there may not be enough: "If I give, I won't have enough for myself." That is such a strong notion that it can also affect your zazen: "If I give everything to this very moment, I won't have enough for the next." And yet the amazing thing is that when you give freely with no fear or expectation, there never is any lack. Only when you begin to hold back does there seem not to be enough. The supply of Dharma is endless if you are willing to function as a conduit. Anytime somebody turns on the tap, it flows out of you. This requires great courage and faith, for you may feel you never have enough, even though in every moment you are always receiving exactly what you need.

If you are not getting enough love and attention, you can take it as a sign that you need to be more generous. When you give yourself completely away in each moment, the feeling of not getting enough won't arise. If you take giving as your practice, it will be true generosity even if you benefit from it, and your family and others will learn the value of generosity. What better gift can you give to those you love? Even if you only possess a trace of generosity, you will have joy in your heart. When you give of yourself, either through work or material things, you feel better about yourself. Generosity and faith in the Way is what you should transmit to others. The possibility of this transmission is due to the merit and functioning of the Buddha. It is worthwhile even to practice one of the actions of the Bodhisattva.

You cannot change the mind of a single person, but if you give generously you have the opportunity to show the heart of the Buddha and lead others to liberation. In order to do this, you should take the first step to total and complete enlightenment, which is to begin being generous. Generosity is the first of the six *paramitas* of the Bodhisattva; of all the six *paramitas*, *dana paramita* is the most direct path to liberation. Mind cannot be measured, whether it be great or small, nor can you measure the size of giving.

Bodhisattvas offer their lives to serving the Buddha, Dharma, and Sangha. You cannot be liberated without relinquishing the self. Giving can change your whole perspective on life. Everything in the world is created in the mind. Just by shifting the mind, you can change the whole world.

Notes

[1] Rinzai, 28.
[2] Maezumi and Loori.
[3] Maezumi Roshi translation, unpublished.

The Four Benevolent Ways of the Bodhisattva
Loving and Compassionate Speech

—·—·—·—·—·—◈—·—·—·—·—·—

Loving speech means that whenever you see sentient beings,
your compassion is aroused naturally and you use loving words.
You cannot imagine using coarse speech. It is natural to ask about
another's welfare when you greet him. In Buddhism you use the
word chincho *(to take care of yourself) and for older people there*
is the greeting fushin *(how are you?) When you meet together and*
talk, you should care for each other, as you would do for a baby.
With such a mind, you can speak truly—that is to say, you can
speak compassionately. If someone has virtue you should praise it,
and if they do not you should feel pity. If you love compassionate
words, the action of loving words will increase. The compassionate
words that are concealed in your daily life will emerge. Throughout
life, in the present time, you should seek to speak compassionately.
This doesn't mean seeking loving words from others, but giving
them from your own hearts. You should never forget compassionate
words either in this world or the next; they are the basis of the next
life. To become friends with the enemy and to reconcile enemy
kings should be the root of compassionate words. When you listen

to loving words, you should face others, and that will make them happy and make them smile with joy. If you listen to loving words fully, you will impress your heart and spirit. You should realize that loving words come from the mind of love and that this mind is based on compassion. You should learn that loving words have great power to change situations and that they have greater virtue and meaning than mere praise.

When Bodhi-mind has been awakened, it functions as compassion. Whenever you meet a person, your compassion is aroused naturally. With Bodhi-mind, you do not hold back. When the situation calls for loving words, you give them freely and you do not speak harshly. When the situation calls for harsh words, you give them compassionately.

Bodhi-mind has little to do with our conventional understanding of speaking the truth. Buddhas and Bodhisattvas know they are lying. Ultimately there is no Truth, only endless layers of self-deception. The deluded think they are speaking the truth, but to speak the Truth, one must first awaken to the Truth. Ordinary people want to be truthful but they are often deceiving themselves because they only see one side of the truth at a time. Awakened people cannot speak other than the Truth, for whatever they say is the Buddha-dharma. Even their criticism and insults are compassionate speech. But only a Buddha realizes this, whereas the ordinary person cannot grasp it.

Master Rinzai said:

What are you so hotly chasing? Putting another head on top of your head, you blind idiots; your head is right where it should be. What are you lacking? Followers of the Way, the one functioning right in front of your eyes is no different from the Buddhas and the Patriarchs, but you do not realize it, so you turn to the outside to seek. Do not be deceived! If you turn to the outside, there is no Truth; neither is there anything to be obtained from the inside. Rather than attaching yourselves to words and letters, better calm down and seek nothing further. Do not cling to what has come to be in the past, nor long for what has not yet come to be in the future. This is better than ten years' pilgrimage. As I see it, there is nothing complicated. Just be your ordinary selves in an ordinary life, wear your robes and eat your food, and having nothing further to seek, peacefully pass your time.[1]

When you drop the dualistic way of viewing the world and stop seeing anything or anyone as other than yourself, that is called *prajna*, the wisdom that goes beyond all distinctions. The functioning of *prajna* is compassion. That compassion can have a sharp edge, cutting right through self-clinging, and may look cruel and heartless at times. An ancient master once said, "To guard and maintain the essential teachings of Buddhism must be the vocation of the noble soul. He does not blink when killing a man, and then the man may be instantly enlightened."[2] A true teacher functions freely, creating situations that bring about awakening. It is all just action and reaction, responding in the moment. There is no separate person involved. The life-giving sword and the killing sword both come directly out of concern for the well-being of all sentient beings.

Everything has its proper function and position, its place in this world. For example, when you are about to enter the meditation hall and take off your shoes, why not arrange them neatly? Something is wrong if things are left in disarray, and you still wonder why your life is chaotic and not going well. If the space you live in is kept clean and orderly, it helps the mind to settle. In a way it is easier to treat everything with respect if you own less. Then you appreciate more what you have and take better care of it. If you have only as much space and furniture as you really use, then it is possible to give it all proper attention. Carelessness means not having a loving heart, lacking the incentive to treat everything with the love and respect it deserves.

You should show respect and give praise to those who have virtue and feel pity for those who do not. To be respectful is not something that requires "enlightenment." You just have to stop being self-centered and greedy. If you must be greedy, best to be greedy to express compassion! If you don't develop the kind of open and flexible mind that simply sees what needs to be done and does it, you may have a difficult time attaining enlightenment. Enlightenment is not something separate and apart from compassion. It is just how you are in every moment. Only by going through suffering yourself do you start to empathize with others.

Sometimes during sitting it feels as if nothing is happening. In one sense that is true, but on the other hand the attachment to self lessens and the heart has a chance to open. Being beaten by zazen, you become more humble. Going through both physical and mental pain allows your heart to open to all suffering sentient beings, to everyone and everything.

It is not a matter of understanding something. Intellectual knowledge is such a shallow thing anyway. You may never understand as much as some scientists, but that doesn't necessarily mean that their hearts are more open. Go to university, get a Ph.D., learn about the workings of the whole universe—it probably won't open your heart. But sit for one week or three months, experience your own pain, and your heart opens.

Working intimately with a teacher, students discover their self-centeredness and come face-to-face with their fear, anger, greed, and arrogance. Most people ignore their dark side, not purposely, but because they are so busy and self-involved that there is no opportunity for them to take a good look at themselves. Sitting in zazen, we are facing our egocentricity continuously, and we should be grateful to be able to see it. It is not easy, but how can we ever take care of this great matter of life and death if we don't even know how greedy and self-centered we are?

If we harbor hatred and resentment, we are the ones who get hurt the most. There are people who try to preserve the memory of the Holocaust so that it will never happen again. This is understandable, but keeping the hatred alive is exactly what will bring about a repetition of such a tragedy. That is how karma works. If you hurt me and I keep hating you, you will continue to hurt me. When you die, it will be your children who hate me. This can go on generation after generation; it usually takes two to keep the hatred going. No one who hangs on to hatred and grudges is ever going to be at peace.

If we really communicate with one another, compassion will spread and increase; but if we are too busy, then there is no time for kind words. It is easier to have goals and ambitions than to open one's heart. Opening the heart is what the quality of the next life depends upon, and not just after physical death. Our next life is the very next moment. Every moment we are dying and being reborn. Just as every new moment is dependent on the moment before, our future existence is also dependent on how we behaved in the past.

Receiving and giving work together—one cannot function without the other. Only taking doesn't work; neither does only giving. You must be able to do both. An interesting way to look at giving and receiving is to remember that you don't just breathe in. If you were really greedy, you would only inhale. Fortunately, all of us are born with the innate Buddha wisdom not only to inhale but also to exhale. Twenty-four hours a day you practice the wisdom of breathing in and breathing out. You all have that wisdom; every living thing has it. Following your breath is finding your spirit. Breathing in and out is what the spirit is; the word spirit means breath. Breath is life. Without breathing, you would be a corpse. When you expire, breathe out your last breath, the spirit is gone.

Notes

[1] Rinzai, 22.
[2] *Hekiganroku*, Case 5, Master Engo's Introduction, Sekida, 158–59.

The Four Benevolent Ways of the Bodhisattva
Beneficial Action

---◆---

Beneficial action means that you take care of every kind of person, no matter whether of high or low position, for this gives your life merit. You should think about people's present and future and about taking care of them so that they will develop merit.

A long time ago, during the Shin era in China, there was a man named Koyu who, on seeing a fisherman catch a turtle, bought it and released it in the river. In the Gokan period, there was a man called Yoho, who, as a boy, saved a sparrow at the foot of Mount Kain. When these people saw the turtle and the sparrow, they simply felt sorry; they did not expect any special merit. They could not stop themselves from helping; their beneficial intent simply caused them to do so.

Beneficial action is the functioning of compassion and naturally arises out of *prajna* wisdom. Someone who has awakened to this wisdom makes no distinction between people of high or low position, and does not covet some just because they are rich and famous, nor shun others just because they are poor and destitute. What arises naturally out of Bodhi-mind is the aspiration to awaken sentient beings both in the present and the future, and to make sure that they will grow in the Way.

People are looking for meaning in life, but will only find it by rising above the egoistic self and devoting themselves to some greater purpose. Nothing belongs to the self and yet everyone is able to give endlessly. We are born with a limitless capacity for giving. Everyone has something to give. Having a life, we can always give that. In Zen practice, one finds meaning by forgetting the self and serving all beings.

Dogen Zenji says that all the Patriarchs are Bodhisattvas and the point is to realize that you too are a Bodhisattva. Zen practice is to go where people are. Kanzeon appears as anything or anybody in order to liberate sentient beings, even as a child, as a drunkard on the street, or a dog. How can that be? How can a dog be a Bodhisattva? How can a baby be one? Actually it is easier for a dog or a baby to be a Bodhisattva than for an ordinary person. At least dogs and babies have not misplaced their Buddha-nature as ordinary people have. A dog is just a dog and a baby is just a baby. Are you just yourself? This is the point. Until you can be just yourself, you are not a Bodhisattva.

Master Rinzai said: "Venerable ones, just be your ordinary selves and refrain from fanciful imaginings. There are old bald-heads who cannot tell true from false. They see gods and devils; they point to the east or indicate the west; they fancy fine weather or are fond of rain; and so they carry on and on. One day they will have to face Yama (Judge of the Dead) to repay their debts and swallow red-hot iron balls. For men and women, misled by the antics of such wild fox sprites, get entangled in their fables. Blind old fools! The day is sure to come when they will have to pay back the cost of their keep."[1]

The actions of Bodhisattvas are sometimes difficult to understand from a conventional perspective of right and wrong. Interpretations of their compassionate actions that come through the filter of the dualistic mind are often mistaken and can be very destructive. In order to bring even one person to complete awakening, a Buddha is willing to sacrifice everything: home, family, reputation, financial security, position, and even his own life. Ordinary people have a difficult time conceiving of such beneficial action. To their way of thinking, the end does not justify the means. To the awakened person, however, often the end justifies the means, if the end is the enlightenment of others. These two minds, the mind of an ordinary person and the mind of an awakened person, cannot meet. For Bodhisattvas, more important than anything else is to awaken others to the One Buddha-mind.

Foolish people think that if the other person's merit comes first, their own will lose out, but this is not true. Beneficial action is the one principle wherein you find no opposition between subject and object. It is a deed which gives merit to both.

Foolish people think that if they put others first then somehow they will lose out. Afraid that there is not going to be enough love, money, etc., they are continuously seeking for more, dissatisfied and suffering. When people cease being foolish, they become more generous, giving freely of love, money, etc. They have nothing further to seek; this is why they are fulfilled and not suffering.

Beneficial action is the one principle coming out of compassion which finds no opposition between self and others. This kind of action benefits both others and oneself. No matter how much you give, you will never run short. If you help others accomplish the Way, your own capacity only expands. You discover your limitless capacity to give.

A Bodhisattva tells others to go ahead and wants everyone to clarify the Way. He doesn't remain on top of the mountain, but comes down where ordinary people dwell. Everyone can be a Bodhisattva by raising the Bodhi-mind and being generous.

There is a story from ancient times about King Shu. If a guest came when he was taking a bath or eating a meal, he would straighten his hair and receive the guest. He tried his best to give his merit to others without discriminating between people of different countries. He treated everyone in the same way. He took care of all people alike, no matter whether they bore him a grudge or were friendly.

If you do not have any discrimination, you can produce merit both for yourself and others. If you have such a mind, you can find it in natural phenomena such as grass, trees, wind and water. This mind should be resolved and always produce merit. Naturally such beneficial intent considers foolish people and wishes to save them.

A Bodhisattva is always ready to put whatever he is doing aside to serve others, welcoming everyone without discrimination. He doesn't cling to his personal self; this is why his own interests do not come first. The unenlightened cannot conceive of this. They think a Bodhisattva can pick his actions and who will benefit from them. Because ordinary people can choose whether they give or not, they think that giving can be controlled. Only when it comes from a dualistic mind can generosity be turned on and off. The Bodhisattva cannot turn it on and off, because his whole being is giving, so every action is the Dharma; he cannot choose who benefits either. Everybody is benefiting from a Bodhisattva's action, even if they don't appreciate it.

When you do not have any discrimination in your mind, you produce immense merit for yourself and others. When you have such a mind, you can appreciate everything as the Buddha, even grasses, trees, wind and water. This mind is always resolved to pursue the Way and produces merit. It is only natural that an awakened mind considers the folly of foolish people and wishes to bring them to liberation. It is out of this concern that Dogen Zenji came to the West.

Notes

[1] Rinzai, 8.

The Four Benevolent Ways of the Bodhisattva
Identification with Others

Identification with others means not to differentiate self from others, in the manner of Shakyamuni, who was born and spent his whole life as a human being. He spent his entire life identifying with others, even in other worlds such as hells or the animal realms. When you identify with others, you are at one with yourself and others. There is an expression to be friends with the koto [Japanese musical instrument], poetry, and sake. This means that as a human being you make friends with such things as music, poetry, and sake, and that they make friends with you. At times, you harmonize first with yourself, and, at times, first with others. The relationship between yourself and others is as endless as is your relationship with time.

Identification with others means not to differentiate between self and others. Believing you are separate is called delusion. Realizing you are not separate is called enlightenment. Getting stuck in this realization is called being deluded within enlightenment. Going beyond that stuckness is called being enlightened beyond enlightenment. No longer having any such foolish notions as one or two, with not even a trace of enlightenment remaining, is delusion within delusion, the sanity of Tantra.

The Buddha spent his whole life not separating himself from others. Wherever he went, whether it be to the highest heavens or down to the deepest hells, he was completely one with each situation. This is the functioning of a Bodhisattva. The Buddha, who is a great Bodhisattva, appears as the lowest of the low when necessary in order to liberate sentient beings. There is no place that he would not go and nothing he would not do in order to awaken even a single being. The Buddha is ready to give up his life for the sake of others. His freedom to do so arose from his willingness to go through the pain and suffering that are the gateway to complete awakening. It is only through your willingness to surrender yourself to your own suffering and that of others that you can truly be called a follower of the Way.

Dogen Zenji's teaching is the Supreme Vehicle (*Saijojo*) and goes beyond the Three *Yanas*. It includes and yet transcends Hinayana, Mahayana, and Buddhayana; it is the Tantra of Zen. Dogen Zenji was very critical of practices that didn't embrace all the aspects of the Buddha-dharma. *Saijojo* Zen is the practice of the Buddha-dharma for the sake of the Buddha-dharma alone. It even goes beyond any purpose of liberating oneself or others. Dogen Zenji's practice is about complete relinquishment of one's personal self so that one's life is nothing less than the embodiment of the Buddha-dharma.

The Lesser Vehicle is not necessarily inferior, only partial, and not the Buddha's ultimate teaching. Dogen Zenji's entire life was devoted to the transmission of *Shobo*, the true Dharma, which is all-inclusive. His devotion is a great inspiration to those who wish to transmit the Buddha mind-seal in the Western world.

It is only by forgetting the self that one practices identification with others. When you relinquish, you are in harmony with yourself. Actually, when you surrender the self you discover your true self. This self is no-self and is one with all selves. The relationship between yourself and others is as endless as your relationship with time.

Kanshi said: "The seas accept water without limit, thus creating great oceans, and mountains accept earth without limit, thus forming great mountain ranges."

In such a way, an outstanding king accepts all kinds of people, and thus he will have many people and countries in his rule. Such an outstanding king will become an emperor. An emperor does not dislike people, but this does not mean he will not give punishment or indeed prizes. Even when he punishes, he never dislikes the person he is punishing. Long ago, when people were simple and honest, there was no need for any punishment; things were different from the present. Even in the present day, some people seek the Way without expectation of reward or punishment, though foolish people cannot even imagine such an idea.

An outstanding king has a clear understanding of people's minds, and he does not reject nor discriminate against anyone. In this way, people gather round him, thus forming a country or state. They show the kind of mind which seeks an outstanding king. Average people, however, do not know the idea or principle of the nature of an outstanding king; they are simply happy if the king does not dislike or reject them. Sometimes, not even being aware

*that the king will not reject them, they support him. In other words,
brilliant king and foolish people are able to live in harmony. In this
manner, people [i.e., sentient beings] ask the king [Bodhisattva] for
his support.*

*In all respects and wishes, the Bodhisattva practices in order
to save sentient beings. What is most necessary is that you face
everything with an open and flexible mind. All these four virtues—
generosity, loving and compassionate words, beneficial action, and
identification with others—possess and include each other [i.e.,
they are not independent]. In this way, these virtues total sixteen.*

Bodhi-mind, the awakened mind, is also known as *Dai
Shin,* Big Mind, because it accepts everything and everyone
without limit, as the seas accept water without limit thus creating great oceans, and mountains accept the earth without
limit thus forming great mountain ranges. An outstanding
teacher accepts all students without discrimination, and thus
a large number of people from many countries will wish to
follow him. The Buddha was such an outstanding teacher.
When Buddhas admonish, they don't do it out of hatred, but
out of righteous anger. When they see people acting out of
ignorance or arrogance in such a way as to hurt themselves or
others, they may respond with anger, even scolding or striking them. Even when Buddhas are reprimanding students,
they don't dislike them; their anger is compassion. Buddhas
transmute anger into compassion, as alchemists transmute
lead into gold.

Outstanding students seek the Way without expectation
of reward or punishment, while those with deluded understanding cannot imagine such an idea and are constantly
looking for reward and profit, fearing blame and reproach.

An outstanding teacher has a clear understanding of
people's minds and does not reject or discriminate against

anyone. He puts up no boundaries between himself and others. Therefore, people gather around him to practice zazen single-mindedly and form a harmonious community. Those with great aspiration seek an outstanding teacher. For this reason they put aside all petty notions and secondary matters, realizing the wisdom of no-escape. Those with deluded understanding, however, may not always recognize the wisdom of a true Bodhisattva and may be deceived by those who fit their deluded picture.

However it may appear, a Bodhisattva's life is the manifestation of his desire to awaken sentient beings. He doesn't need to do anything special and has no particular intention. As a Bodhisattva, it is most necessary that you face everything with an open and flexible mind.

The ten thousand dharmas appear, and the ten thousand dharmas are not other than your own mind. The four virtues—generosity, loving and compassionate speech, beneficial action, and identification with others—are nothing but the functioning of Bodhi-mind. They are not four separate virtues, but contains the other three. They are not independent, but work in complete harmony, indivisible from one another.

As Dogen Zenji says in the "Genjokoan":

> When the ten thousand dharmas are seen as the Buddha-dharma, then there is enlightenment and delusion, practice, birth and death, Buddhas and ordinary people. When the ten thousand dharmas are without self, then there is no delusion and no enlightenment, no Buddhas and no ordinary people, no birth and no death. The Buddha Way goes beyond being and nonbeing. Therefore, there is birth and death, delusion and enlightenment, Buddhas and ordinary people.

Nevertheless, with our attachments flowers fall, and weeds spring up with our aversion.

To practice and confirm all things while maintaining oneself is delusion. That all things advance and realize the self is enlightenment. Thus it is Buddhas who enlighten delusion and it is ordinary people who are deluded in enlightenment. Further, there are those who attain enlightenment beyond enlightenment, and there are those who are deluded within delusion. When Buddhas are truly Buddhas they are not particularly aware of being Buddha. However, one who is a realized Buddha further advances in realizing Buddha and this traceless enlightenment continues endlessly."[1]

Those who are deluded within delusion go far beyond sanity and madness.

Notes

[1] Based on Maezumi Roshi's translation in Maezumi and Loori, *The Way of Everyday Life*.

Appendix One
Gakudo Yojinshu
Points to Watch in Practicing the Way

Point One: The Need to Awaken to the Bodhi-mind

The Bodhi-mind is known by many names; all refer to the One Mind of the Buddha. The Venerable Nagarjuna said, "The mind that sees into the flux of arising and decaying and recognizes the transient nature of the world is also known as the Bodhi-mind." Why, then, is temporary dependence on this mind called the Bodhi-mind? When the transient nature of the world is recognized, the ordinary selfish mind does not arise; neither does the mind that seeks for fame and profit.

Aware that time waits for no man, train as though you were attempting to save your head from being enveloped in flames. Reflecting on the transient nature of body and life, exert yourself just as the Buddha Shakyamuni did when he raised his foot.

Although you hear the flattering call of the god Kimnara and the kalavinka bird, pay no heed, regarding them

227

as merely the evening breeze blowing in your ears. Even though you see a face as beautiful as that of Mao-ch'ang or Hsi-shih, think of them as merely the morning dew blocking your vision.

When freed from the bondage of sound, color, and shape, you will naturally become one with the true Bodhi-mind. Since ancient times there have been those who have heard little of true Buddhism and others who have seen little of the sutras. Most of them have fallen into the pitfall of fame and profit, losing the essence of the Way forever. What a pity! How regrettable! This should be well understood.

Even though you have read the expedient or true teachings of excellent sutras or transmitted the esoteric and exoteric teachings, unless you forsake fame and profit you cannot be said to have awakened to the Bodhi-mind.

There are some who say that the Bodhi-mind is the highest supreme enlightenment of the Buddha, free from fame and profit. Others say that it is that which embraces the one billion worlds in a single moment of thought, or that it is the teaching that not a single delusion arises. Still others say that it is the mind that directly enters into the realm of the Buddha. These people, not yet understanding what the Bodhi-mind is, wantonly slander it. They are indeed far from the Way.

Reflect on your ordinary mind, selfishly attached as it is to fame and profit. Is it endowed with the essence and appearance of the three thousand worlds in a single moment of thought? Has it experienced the teaching that not a single delusion arises? No, there is nothing there but the delusion of fame and profit, nothing worthy of being called the Bodhi-mind.

Although there have been Patriarchs since ancient times

who have used secular means to realize enlightenment, none of them has been attached to fame and profit, or even Buddhism, let alone the ordinary world.

The Bodhi-mind is, as previously mentioned, that which recognizes the transient nature of the world—one of the four insights. It is utterly different from that referred to by madmen.

The non-arising mind and the appearance of the one billion worlds are fine practices after having awakened to the Bodhi-mind. "Before" and "after," however, should not be confused. Simply forget the self and quietly practice the Way. This is truly the Bodhi-mind.

The sixty-two viewpoints are based on self; so when egoistic views arise, just do zazen quietly, observing them. What is the basis of your body, its inner and outer possessions? You received your body, hair, and skin from your parents. The two droplets, red and white, of your parents, however, are empty from beginning to end; hence there is no self here. Mind, discriminating consciousness, knowledge, and dualistic thought bind life. What, ultimately, are exhaling and inhaling? They are not self. There is no self to be attached to. The deluded, however, are attached to self, while the enlightened are unattached. But still you seek to measure the self that is no self, and attach yourselves to arisings that are nonarising, neglecting to practice the Way. By failing to sever your ties with the world, you shun the true teaching and run after the false. Dare you say you are not acting mistakenly?

Point Two: The Need for Training Upon Encountering the True Law

A king's mind can often be changed as the result of advice given by a loyal retainer. If the Buddhas and Patriarchs offer even a single word, there will be none who remain unconverted. Only wise kings, however, heed the advice of their retainers, and only exceptional trainees listen to the Buddha's words.

It is impossible to sever the source of transmigration without casting away the delusive mind. In the same way, if a king fails to heed the advice of his retainers, virtuous policy will not prevail, and he will be unable to govern the country well.

Point Three: The Need to Realize the Way Through Constant Training

Lay people believe that government office can be acquired as a result of study. The Buddha Shakyamuni teaches, however, that training encompasses enlightenment. I have never heard of anyone who became a government official without study or realized enlightenment without training.

Although it is true that different training methods exist—those based on faith or the Law—the sudden or gradual realization of enlightenment—still one realizes enlightenment as a result of training. In the same way, although the depth of people's learning differs, as does their speed of comprehension, government office is acquired through accumulated study. None of these things depends on whether the rulers are superior or not, or whether one's luck is good or bad.

If government office could be acquired without study, who could transmit the method by which the former king successfully ruled the nation? If enlightenment could be realized without training, who could understand the teaching of the Tathagata, distinguishing, as it does, the difference between delusion and enlightenment? Understand that although you train in the world of delusion, enlightenment is already there. Then, for the first time, you will realize that boats and rafts [the sutras] are but yesterday's dream and will be able to sever forever the old views that bound you to them.

The Buddha does not force this understanding on you. Rather, it comes naturally from your training in the Way, for training invites enlightenment. Your own treasure does not come from the outside. Since enlightenment is one with training, enlightened action leaves no traces. Therefore, when looking back on training with enlightened eyes, you will find there is no illusion to be seen, just as white clouds extending for ten thousand *ri* cover the whole sky.

When enlightenment is harmonized with training, you cannot step on even a single particle of dust. Should you be able to do so, you will be as far removed from enlightenment as heaven is from earth. If you return to your true self, you can transcend even the status of the Buddha.

Point Four: The Need for Selfless Practice of the Way

In the practice of the Way it is necessary to accept the true teachings of our predecessors, setting aside our own preconceived notions. The Way cannot be realized with mind or without it. Unless the mind of constant practice is one with the Way, neither body nor mind will know peace. When the body and mind are not at peace, they become obstacles to enlightenment.

How are constant practice and the Way to be harmonized? To do so the mind must neither be attached to nor reject anything; it must be completely free from attachment to fame and profit. One does not undergo Buddhist training in order to gain a good reputation. The minds of Buddhist trainees, like those of most people these days, however, are far from understanding the Way. They do that which others praise, even though they know it to be false. On the other hand, they do not practice that which others scorn, even though they know it to be the true Way. How regrettable!

Reflect quietly on whether your mind and actions are one with the Buddha-dharma or not. If you do so, you will realize how shameful they are. The penetrating eyes of the Buddhas and Patriarchs are constantly illuminating the entire universe.

Since Buddhist trainees do not do anything for the sake of themselves, how could they do anything for the sake of fame and profit? You should train for the sake of the Buddha-dharma alone. The various Buddhas do not show deep compassion for all sentient beings for either their own or others' sakes. This is the Buddhist tradition.

Observe how even animals and insects nurture their young, enduring various hardships in the process. The parents stand to gain nothing by their actions, even after their offspring have reached maturity. Yet, though they are only small creatures, they have deep compassion for their young. This is also the case with regard to the various Buddhas' compassion for all sentient beings. The excellent teachings of these various Buddhas, however, are not limited to compassion alone; rather, they appear in countless ways throughout the universe. This is the essence of the Buddha-dharma.

We are already the children of the Buddha; therefore we should follow in his footsteps. Trainees, do not practice the Buddha-dharma for your own benefit, for fame and profit, or for rewards and miraculous powers. Simply practice the Buddha-dharma for its own sake; this is the true Way.

Point Five: The Need to Seek a True Master

A former Patriarch once said, "If the Bodhi-mind is untrue, all one's training will come to nothing." This saying is indeed true. Furthermore, the quality of the disciple's training depends upon the truth or falsity of his master.

The Buddhist trainee can be compared to a fine piece of timber, and a true master to a good carpenter. Even quality wood will not show its fine grain unless it is worked on by a good carpenter. Even a warped piece of wood will, if handled by a good carpenter, soon show the results of good craftsmanship. The truth or falsity of enlightenment depends upon whether or not one has a true master. This should be well understood.

In our country, however, there have not been any true masters since ancient times. We can tell this by looking at their words, just as we can tell the nature of the source of a river by scooping up some of its water downstream.

For centuries masters in this country have compiled books, taught disciples, and led both human and celestial beings. Their words, however, were still green, still unripe, for they had not yet reached the ultimate in training. They had not yet reached the sphere of enlightenment. Instead, they merely transmitted words and made others recite names and letters. Day and night they counted the treasure of others, without gaining anything for themselves.

These ancient masters must be held responsible for this state of affairs. Some of them taught that enlightenment should be sought outside the mind, others that rebirth in the Pure Land was the goal. Herein lies the source of both confusion and delusion.

Even if good medicine is given to someone, unless that person has also been given the proper directions for taking it the illness may be made worse; in fact, taking medicine may do more harm than taking poison. Since ancient times there have not been any good doctors in our country who were capable of making out the correct prescription or distinguishing between medicine and poison. For this reason it has been extremely difficult to eliminate life's suffering and disease. How, then, can we expect to escape from the sufferings of old age and death?

This situation is completely the fault of the masters, not of the disciples. Why? Because they guide their disciples along the branches of the tree, dispensing with its roots. Before they fully understand the Way themselves, they devote themselves solely to their own egoistic minds, luring others into the world of delusion. How regrettable it is that even these masters are unaware of their own delusion. How can their disciples be expected to know the difference between right and wrong?

Unfortunately, the true Buddha-dharma has not yet spread to this peripheral little country, and true masters have yet to be born. If you want to study the supreme Way, you have to visit masters in faraway Sung China, and reflect there on the true road that is far beyond the delusive mind. If you are unable to find a true master, it is best not to study Buddhism at all. True masters are those who have realized the true Dharma and received the seal of a genuine master. It has nothing to do with their age. For them neither learning nor knowledge is of primary importance. Possessing extraordinary power and influence, they do not rely on selfish views or cling to any obsession, for they have perfectly harmonized knowledge and practice. These are the characteristics of a true master.

Point Six: Advice for the Practice of Zen

The study of the Way through the practice of zazen is of vital importance. You should not neglect it or treat it lightly. In China there are the excellent examples of former Zen masters who cut off their arms or fingers. Long ago the Buddha Shakyamuni renounced both his home and his kingdom—another fine trace of the practice of the Way. If you devote yourself to one thing exclusively and consider it to be training, even lying down will become tedious. If one thing becomes tedious, all things become tedious. You should know that those who like easy things are, as a matter of course, unworthy of the practice of the Way.

Our great teacher, Shakyamuni, was unable to gain the teaching that prevails in the present world until after he had undergone severe training for countless ages in the past. Considering how dedicated the founder of Buddhism was, can his descendants be any less so? Those who seek the Way should not look for easy training. Should you do so, you will never be able to reach the true world of enlightenment or find the treasure house. Even the most gifted of the former Patriarchs have said that the Way is difficult to practice. You should realize how deep and immense Buddhism is. If the Way were, originally, so easy to practice and understand, these former gifted Patriarchs would not have stressed its difficulty. By comparison with the former Patriarchs, people of today do not amount to even as much as a single hair in a herd of nine cows! That is to say, even if these moderns, lacking as they do both ability and knowledge, exert themselves to the utmost, their imagined difficult practice would still be incomparable to that of the former Patriarchs.

Beyond Sanity and Madness

What is the easily practiced and easily understood
teaching of which present-day man is so fond? It is neither a
secular teaching nor a Buddhist one. It is even inferior to the
practice of demons and evil spirits, as well as to that of non-
Buddhist religions and *sravakas* and *pratyekabuddhas*. It may
be said to be the great delusion of ordinary men and women.
Although they imagine that they have escaped from the delusive world, they have, on the contrary, merely subjected
themselves to endless transmigration.

Breaking one's bones and crushing the marrow to gain
Buddhism are thought to be difficult practices. It is still more
difficult, however, to control the mind, let alone undergo prolonged austerities and pure training, while controlling one's
physical actions is most difficult of all.

If the crushing of one's bones were of value, the many
who endured this training in the past should have realized
enlightenment; but in fact, only a few did. If the practice of
austerities were of value, the many who have done so since
ancient times also should have become enlightened; but here,
too, only a few did. This all stems from the great difficulty of
controlling the mind. In Buddhism neither a brilliant mind
nor scholastic understanding is of primary importance. The
same holds true for intellect, volition, consciousness, memory,
imagination, and contemplation. None of these are of any use,
for the Way may be entered only through the harmonization
of body and mind.

The Buddha Shakyamuni said, "Turning the sound-perceiving stream of the mind inward, forsake knowing and
being known." This is what harmonizing body and mind
means. The two qualities of movement and nonmovement
have not appeared at all; this is true harmony.

If it were possible to enter the Way on the basis of hav-ing a brilliant mind and wide knowledge, high-ranking Jinshu should certainly have been able to do so. If common birth were an obstacle to entering the Way, how did Eno become one of the Chinese Patriarchs? These examples clearly show that the process of transmitting the Way does not depend on either a brilliant mind or wide knowledge. In seeking the true Dharma, reflect on yourselves and train diligently.

Neither youth nor age is an obstacle to entering the Way. Joshu was more than sixty years old when he first began to practice, yet he became an outstanding Patriarch. Tei's daughter, on the other hand, was only thirteen years old, but she had already attained a deep understanding of the Way, so much so that she became one of the finest trainees in her monastery.

The majesty of Buddhism appears according to whether or not the effort is made, and differs according to whether or not training with a teacher is involved.

Those who have long devoted themselves to the study of the sutras, as well as those who are well versed in secular learning, should visit a Zen monastery. There are many exam-ples of those who have done so. Nangaku Eshi was a man of many talents, yet he trained under Bodhidharma. Yoka Genkaku was the finest of men; still he trained under Daikan Eno. The clarification of the Dharma and the realization of the Way are dependent upon the power gained from training under Zen masters.

When visiting a Zen master to seek instruction, listen to his teaching without trying to make it conform to your own self-centered viewpoint; otherwise you will be unable to understand what he is saying. Purifying your own body and mind, eyes and ears, simply listen to his teaching, expelling any other thought. Unify your body and mind and receive the master's teaching as if water were being poured from one vessel into another. If you do so, then for the first time you will be able to understand his teaching.

At present, there are some foolish people who either devote themselves to memorizing the words and phrases of the sutras or attach themselves to that which they have heard before. Having done so, they try to equate these with the teachings of a living master. Their minds are filled with their personal views and ancient sayings. They will never be able to become one with their teacher's words. Still others, attaching primary importance to their own self-centered thinking, open the sutras and memorize a word or two, imagining this to be the Buddha-dharma. Later when they are taught the Dharma by an enlightened Zen master, they regard his teaching as true if it corresponds with their own views; otherwise they regard it as false. Not knowing how to give up this mistaken way of thinking, they are unable to return to the true Way. They are to be pitied, for they will remain deluded for countless kalpas. How regrettable!

Buddhist trainees should realize that the Buddha-dharma is beyond either thought, discrimination, and imagination, or insight, perception, and intellectual understanding. Were it not so, why is it that, having been endowed with these various faculties since birth, you have still not realized the Way?

Thought, discrimination, and so forth should be avoided in the practice of the Way. This will become clear if, using thought and so on, you examine yourself carefully. The gateway to the Truth is known only to enlightened Zen masters, not to their learned counterparts.

Point Seven: The Need for Zen Training in Buddhist Practice and Enlightenment

Buddhism is superior to any other teaching. It is for this reason that many people pursue it. During the Tathagata's lifetime, there was only one teaching and only one teacher. The Great Master alone led all beings with his supreme Wisdom. Since the Venerable Mahakasyapa transmitted the Eye Storehouse of the true Dharma, twenty-eight generations in India, six generations in China, and the various patriarchs of the five Zen schools have transmitted it without interruption. Since the P'u-t'ung era [520–526] in the Chinese state of Liang all truly superior individuals—from monks to royal retainers—have taken refuge in Zen Buddhism.

Truly, excellence should be loved because of its excellence. One should not love dragons as Sekko did. In the various countries east of China the casting net of scholastic Buddhism has been spread over the seas and mountains. Even though spread over the mountains, however, it does not contain the heart of the clouds; even though spread over the seas, it lacks the heart of the waves. The foolish are fond of this kind of Buddhism. They are delighted by it like those who take the eye of a fish to be a pearl, or those who treasure a stone from Mount Yen in the belief that it is a precious jewel. Many such people fall into the pit of demons, thereby losing their true Self.

The situation in remote countries like this one is truly regrettable; for here, where the winds of false teachings blow freely, it is difficult to spread the true Dharma. China, however, has already taken refuge in the true Buddha-dharma. Why is it, then, that it has not yet spread to either our country or Korea? Although in Korea at least the name of the true

Dharma can be heard, in our country even this is impossible. This is because the many teachers who went to study the Buddha-dharma in China in the past clung to the net of scholastic Buddhism. Although they transmitted various Buddhist texts, they seem to have forgotten the spirit of Buddhism. Of what value was this? In the end it came to nothing. This is all because they did not know the essence of studying the Way. How regrettable it is that they worked so hard their whole life to no purpose.

When you first enter the gateway of the Buddha-dharma and begin to study the Way, simply listen to the teaching of a Zen master and train accordingly. At that time you should know the following: the Dharma turns self, and self turns the Dharma. When self turns the Dharma, self is strong and the Dharma is weak. In the reverse case, the Dharma is strong and self is weak. Although Buddhism has had these two aspects since long ago, they have only been known by those who have received the true transmission. Without a true master, it is impossible to hear even the names of these two aspects.

Unless one knows the essence of studying the Way, it is impossible to practice it; for how, otherwise, could one determine what is right and what is wrong? Those who now study the Way through the practice of zazen naturally transmit this essence. This is why there have been no mistakes made in the transmission, something that cannot be said of the other Buddhist sects. Those who seek the Buddha-dharma cannot realize the true Way without the practice of zazen.

Point Eight: The Conduct of Zen Monks

Since the time of the Buddha, the twenty-eight

Patriarchs in India and the six in China have directly transmitted the Dharma, adding not even so much as a thread or hair, or allowing even a particle of dust to penetrate it. With the transmission of the Buddha's *kesa* to the Sixth Patriarch, Eno, the Buddha-dharma spread throughout the world. At present the Tathagata's treasury of the true Dharma is flourishing in China. It is impossible to realize what the Dharma is by groping or searching for it. Those who have seen the Way forget their knowledge of it, transcending relative consciousness.

Eno lost his face [his deluded self] while training on Mount Huang-mei. The Second Patriarch, Eka, showed his earnestness by cutting off his arm in front of Bodhidharma's cave, realizing the Buddha-dharma through this action and turning his delusive mind into enlightenment. Thereafter, he prostrated himself before Bodhidharma in deep respect before returning to his original position. Thus did he realize absolute freedom, dwelling in neither body nor mind, nonattached, unlimited.

A monk asked Joshu, "Does a dog have the Buddha-nature?" Joshu replied "*Mu!*" This word *mu* can be neither measured nor grasped, for there is nothing to grab hold of. I would suggest that you try letting go! Then ask yourself these questions: What are body and mind? What is Zen conduct? What are birth and death? What is the Buddha-dharma? What are worldly affairs? And what ultimately are mountains, rivers, and earth, or people, animals, and houses?

If you continue to ask these questions, the two aspects—movement and nonmovement—will clearly not appear. This nonappearance, however, does not mean inflexibility. Unfortunately, however, very few people realize this, while many are deluded thereby. Zen trainees can realize this after they have trained for some time. It is my sincere hope, however, that you will not stop training even after you have become fully enlightened.

Point Nine: The Need to Practice in Accordance with the Way

Buddhist trainees should first determine whether or not their practice is headed toward the Way. Shakyamuni, who was able to harmonize and control his body, speech, and mind, sat beneath a bodhi tree doing zazen. Suddenly, upon seeing the morning star, he became enlightened, realizing the highest supreme Way, which is far beyond that of the *sravakas* and *pratyekabuddhas*. The enlightenment that the Buddha realized through his own efforts has been transmitted from Buddha to Buddha without interruption to the present day. How, then, can those who have realized this enlightenment not have become Buddhas? To be headed toward the Way is to know its appearance and how far it extends. The Way lies under the foot of every man. When you become one with the Way you find that it is right where you are, thus realizing perfect enlightenment. If, however, you take pride in your enlightenment, even though it be very deep, it will be no more than partial enlightenment. These are the essential elements of being headed toward the Way.

Present-day trainees strongly desire to see miracles, even though they do not understand how the Way functions. Who of these is not mistaken? They are like a child who, forsaking both his father and his father's wealth, runs away from home. Even though his father is rich, and he, as an only son, would someday inherit it all, he becomes a beggar, searching for his fortune in faraway places. This is truly the case.

To study the Way is to try to become one with it—to forget even a trace of enlightenment. Those who would practice the Way should first of all believe in it. Those who believe in the Way should believe that they have been in the Way from the very beginning, subject to neither delusion, illusive thoughts, and confused ideas nor increase, decrease, and mistaken understanding. Engendering belief like this, clarify the Way and practice accordingly—this is the essence of studying the Way.

The second method of Buddhist training is to cut off the function of discriminating consciousness and turn away from the road of intellectual understanding. This is the manner in which novices should be guided. Thereafter they will be able to let body and mind fall away, freeing themselves from the dualistic ideas of delusion and enlightenment.

In general there are only a very few who believe they are in the Way. If only you believe that you are truly in the Way, you will naturally be able to understand how it functions, as well as the true meaning of delusion and enlightenment. Make an attempt at cutting off the function of discriminating consciousness; then, suddenly, you will have almost realized the Way.

Point Ten: The Direct Realization of the Way

There are two ways to realize enlightenment. One is to train under a true Zen master, listening to his teaching; the other is to do zazen single-mindedly. In the former case you give full play to the discriminating mind, while through the latter, practice and enlightenment are unified. To enter the Way neither of these two methods can be dispensed with.

Everyone is endowed with body and mind, though their

actions inevitably vary, being either strong or weak, brave or cowardly. It is through the daily actions of our body and mind, however, that we directly become enlightened. This is known as the realization of the Way.

There is no need to change our existing body and mind, for the direct realization of the Way simply means to become enlightened through training under a true Zen master. To do this is neither to be bound by old viewpoints nor to create new ones; it is simply to realize the Way.

Appendix Two
Yuibutsu Yobutsu
Only Buddha and Buddha

—··—·—··—··—·—◈◇◈—·—··—··—·—··—

Part One

Buddha-dharma cannot be known by a person. For this reason, since olden times no ordinary person has realized Buddha-dharma; no practitioner of the Lesser Vehicles has mastered Buddha-dharma. Because it is realized by Buddhas alone, it is said, "Only a Buddha and a Buddha can thoroughly master it."

When you realize Buddha-dharma, you do not think, "This is realization just as I expected." Even if you think so, realization invariably differs from your expectation. Realization is not like your conception of it. Accordingly, realization cannot take place as previously conceived. When you realize Buddha-dharma, you do not consider how realization came about. You should reflect on this: What you think one way or another before realization is not a help for realization.

Although realization is not like any of the thoughts preceding it, this is not because such thoughts were actually bad and could not be realization. Past thoughts in themselves were already realization. But since you were seeking elsewhere, you thought and said that thoughts cannot be realization.

However, it is worth noticing that what you think one way or another is not a help for realization. Then you are cautious not to be small-minded. If realization came forth by the power of your prior thoughts, it would not be trustworthy. Realization does not depend on thoughts, but comes forth far beyond them; realization is helped only by the power of realization itself. Know that then there is no delusion, and there is no realization.

Part Two

When you have unsurpassed wisdom, you are called Buddha. When a Buddha has unsurpassed wisdom, it is called unsurpassed wisdom. Not to know what it is like on this path is foolish. What it is like is to be unstained. To be unstained does not mean that you try forcefully to exclude intention or discrimination, or that you establish a state of nonintention. Being unstained cannot be intended or discriminated at all.

Being unstained is like meeting a person and not considering what he looks like. Also it is like not wishing for more color or brightness when viewing flowers or the moon.

Spring has the tone of spring, and autumn has the scene of autumn; there is no escaping it. So when you want spring or autumn to be different from what it is, notice that it can only be as it is. Or when you want to keep spring or autumn as it is, reflect that it has no unchanging nature.

That which is accumulated is without self, and no mental activity has self. The reason is that not one of the four great elements or the five *skandhas* can be understood as self or identified as self, even though you think it is self. Still, when you clarify that there is nothing to be disliked or longed for, then the original face is revealed by your practice of the way.

Part Three

A teacher of old said:

Although the entire universe is nothing but the Dharma body of the self, you should not be hindered by the Dharma body. If you are hindered by the Dharma body, you will not be able to turn freely, no matter how hard you may try. But there should be a way to be free from hindrance. If you cannot say clearly how to free all people, you will soon lose even the life of the Dharma body and sink in the ocean of suffering for a long time.

If you are asked in this way, how can you answer so as to keep the Dharma body alive and avoid sinking in the ocean of suffering?

In that case, say, "The entire universe is the Dharma body of the self." When you say that the entire universe is the Dharma body of the self, words cannot express it. When words cannot express it, should we understand there is nothing to be said? Without words, ancient Buddhas said something.

There is birth in death, and there is death in birth. Death is entirely death, and birth is entirely birth. This is so not because you make it so, but because Dharma is like this. Therefore, when Buddha turns the Dharma wheel, there is insight such as this and expression such as this. Know that it is also like this when Buddha manifests a body to awaken sentient beings. This is called "awareness of no-birth."

"Buddha manifests a body and awakens sentient beings"

means that awakening sentient beings is itself the manifestation of the Buddha body. In the midst of awakening sentient beings, do not pursue manifestation. Seeing manifestation, do not look about for awakening.

Understand that in the midst of awakening sentient beings, the Buddha-dharma is totally experienced. Explain it and actualize it this way. Know that it is the same with manifestation and having the Buddha body.

This is so because "Buddha manifests a body and awakens sentient beings." This principle is clarified in that from the morning of attaining the way until the evening of *parinirvana,* Buddha discoursed freely, without words getting in the way.

Part Four

An ancient Buddha said:

The entire universe is the true human body.
The entire universe is the gate of liberation.
The entire universe is the eye of Vairochana.
The entire universe is the Dharma body of the self.

"The true human body" means your own true body. Know that the entire universe is your own true body, which is not a temporary body.

If someone asks you why we do not usually notice this, say, "Just reflect within yourself that the entire universe is the true human body." Or say, "The entire universe is the true human body—you already know this."

Also, "The entire universe is the gate of liberation" means that you are not at all entangled or captivated. What is called "the entire universe" is undivided from the moment, the ages, mind and words. This limitless and boundless experience is the "entire universe." Even if you seek to enter or go through this gate of liberation, it cannot be done. How is this so? Reflect on the questions raised. If you intend to seek outside what is is, nothing will be attained.

"The entire universe is the eye of Vairochana" means that Buddhas have a single eye. Do not suppose that a Buddha's eye is like those of human beings.

Human beings have two eyes, but when you say "a human eye," you don't say "two eyes" or "three eyes." Those who study the teaching should not understand that "the eye of a Buddha," "the eye of Dharma," or "the celestial eye" is like the two eyes of human beings. To believe that it is like human eyes is lamentable. Understand now that there is only a Buddha's single eye, which is itself the entire universe.

A Buddha may have one thousand eyes or myriad eyes. But presently it is said that the entire universe is the one eye of Vairochana. Therefore, it is not mistaken to say that this eye is one of many eyes of a Buddha, just as it is not mistaken to understand that a Buddha has only one eye. A Buddha indeed has many kinds of eyes—three eyes, one thousand eyes, or eighty-four thousand eyes. Do not be surprised to hear that there are eyes such as these.

Also learn that the entire universe is the Dharma body of the self. To seek to know the self is invariably the wish of living beings. However, those who see the true self are rare. Only Buddhas know the true self.

People outside the way regard what is not the self as the self. But what Buddhas call the self is the entire universe. Therefore, there is never an entire universe that is not the self, with or without our knowing it. On this matter defer to the words of the ancient Buddhas.

Part Five

Long ago a monk asked an old master, "When hundreds, thousands, or myriads of objects come all at once, what should be done?"

The master replied, "Don't try to control them."

What he means is that in whatever way objects come, do not try to change them. Whatever comes is the Buddhadharma, not objects at all. Do not understand the master's reply as merely a brilliant admonition, but realize that it is the truth. Even if you try to control what comes, it cannot be controlled.

Part Six

An ancient Buddha said,"The mountains, rivers, and earth are born at the same moment with each person. All Buddhas of the three worlds are practicing together with each person."

If we look at the mountains, rivers, and earth when a person is born, his birth does not seem to be bringing forth additional mountains, rivers, and earth on top of the existing ones. Yet the ancient Buddha's word cannot be mistaken. How should we understand this? Even if you do not understand it, you should not ignore it. So, be determined to understand it. Since this word is already expounded, you should listen to it. Listen until you understand.

This is how to understand. Is there anyone who knows what his birth in its beginning or end is like? No one knows either birth's end or its beginning; nevertheless everyone is born. Similarly, no one knows the extremities of the mountains, rivers, and earth, but all see this place and walk here. Do not think with regret that the mountains, rivers, and earth are not born with you. Understand that the ancient Buddha teaches that your birth is nonseparate from the mountains, rivers, and earth.

Again, all Buddhas of the three worlds have already practiced, attained the way, and completed realization. How should we understand that those Buddhas are practicing together with us? First of all, examine a Buddha's practice. A Buddha's practice is to practice with all beings, it is not a Buddha's practice. This being so, all Buddhas, from the moment of attaining realization, realize and practice the Way together with the entire universe and all beings.

You may have doubts about this. But the ancient Buddha's word was expounded in order to clarify your confused thinking. Do not think that Buddhas are other than you. According to this teaching, when all Buddhas of the three worlds arouse the thought of enlightenment and practice, they never exclude our body-and-mind. You should understand this. To doubt this is to slander the Buddhas of the three worlds.

When we reflect quietly, it appears that our body-and-mind has practiced together with all Buddhas of the three worlds and has together with them aroused the thought of enlightenment. When we reflect on the past and future of our body-and-mind, we cannot find the boundary of self or others. By what delusion do we believe our body-and-mind is apart from all Buddhas of the three worlds? Such delusion is groundless. How then can delusion hinder the arousing of the thought of enlightenment and the practicing of the Way by all Buddhas of the three worlds? Thus, understand that the Way is not a matter of your knowing or not knowing.

Part Seven

A teacher of old said, "Chopping down is nothing other than chopping down; moving about is beyond discussion. Mountains, rivers, and earth are the entirely revealed body of the Dharma king.

A person of the present should study this phrase of the teacher of old. There is a Dharma king who understands that the body of the Dharma king is not different from chopping down, just as mountains are on earth, and the earth is holding up mountains.

When you understand, a moment of no-understanding does not come and hinder understanding, and understanding does not break no-understanding. Instead, understanding and no-understanding are just like spring and autumn.

However, when you do not understand, the pervasive voice of Dharma does not reach your ears; in the midst of the voice your ears dally about. But when you understand, the voice has already reached your ears; *samadhi* has emerged.

Know that no-understanding cannot be discerned by a self; the Dharma king's understanding is just like this.

In the Dharma king's body the eye is just like the body, and the mind is the same as the body. There is not the slightest gap between mind and body; everything is fully revealed. Similarly, you should understand that in illumination and discourse the Dharma king's body is revealed.

Part Eight

There has been a saying since olden times: "No one except a fish knows a fish's heart, no one except a bird follows a bird's trace."

Yet those who really understand this principle are rare. To think that no one knows a fish's heart or a bird's trace is mistaken. You should know that fish always know one another's heart, unlike people who do not know one another's heart. But when the fish try to go up through the Dragon Gate, they know one another's intention and have the same heart. Or they share the heart of breaking through the Nine Great Bends. Those who are not fish hardly know this.

Again, when a bird flies in the sky, beasts do not even dream of finding or following its trace. As they do not know that there is such a thing, they cannot even imagine this. However, a bird can see traces of hundreds and thousands of small birds having passed in flocks, or traces of so many lines of large birds having flown south or north. Those traces may be even more evident than the carriage tracks left on a road or the hoofprints of a horse seen in the grass. In this way, a bird sees birds' traces.

Buddhas are like this. You may wonder how many lifetimes Buddhas have been practicing. Buddhas, large or small, although they are countless, all know their own traces. You never know a Buddha's trace when you are not a Buddha.

You may wonder why you do not know. The reason is that, while Buddhas see these traces with a Buddha's eye, those who are not Buddhas do not have a Buddha's eye, and just notice the Buddha's attributes.

All who do not know should search out the trace of the Buddha's path. If you find footprints, you should investigate whether they are the Buddha's. On being investigated, the Buddha's trace is known; and whether it is long or short, shallow or deep, is also known. To illuminate your trace is accomplished by studying the Buddha's trace. Accomplishing this is Buddha-dharma.

Appendix Three
Bodaisatta Shishobo
The Four Benevolent Ways of the Bodhisattva

*The four ways a Bodhisattva acts to benefit human beings
are:* fuse (dana), *giving or generosity;* aigo, *loving or compassionate
speech;* rigyo, *beneficial action; and* doji, *identification with others.*

Generosity

Fuse also means *futon,* which is not to covet or be
greedy; not to flatter, adulate, nor curry favor. Even a king
who controls the whole world must have *futon* if he wishes to
propagate the right way. Only by the virtue of *futon* can he
build a peaceful world. The virtue of *futon* is like the virtue
you grant to jewels and to people that you do not know:
without greed or malice. It is the same as offering a flower
that blooms in the far mountains to a Buddha, or offering precious jewels or a previous life to a sentient being. We possess
in our original nature the virtue of generosity, spiritual or
material, in each moment. Although in principle nothing
belongs to self, you can be generous. It is of no concern
whether the gift is large or small: the important point is
whether it can be beneficial to others. The merit of generosity
itself bears fruit. If you entrust and commit yourself to the

Way, you will be complete. In such ways treasure begets treasure, and becomes generosity. You give generously yourself and accordingly others too give generously. The motivating power of giving pierces heavenly beings, human beings, saints and sages, and leads to complete enlightenment. This is due to *innen* (causal motivation) for generous actions.

The Buddha said that when a donor comes to an assembly of monks, they will look respectfully at him. The meaning of this is that you do not look at the mind of the person who gives. One can touch the mind without words so you should be generous. One could give a single word or a verse of teaching to people, a small coin, or even a blade of grass. Such generosity can cause good deeds in this world and the next. The Dharma is a treasure, and treasure is the Dharma. This is due to the compassion of Bodhisattvas.

The following is an example of this:

There once was a king who tried to cure a sick minister by giving him medicine and burning his own beard. The people of his country trusted him. Also there was a child who, playing in a sand box, offered sand as food to the Buddha. Later due to the merit of the action the king ascended to the throne, for in both cases they both did what they could without expecting results.

Supplying a boat on the river or building a bridge are deeds of generosity. If you learn the real meaning of giving, you will know that to have a position in society and to act on behalf of society is also generosity. Politics and industry are themselves forms of giving. It is their nature just as when the time comes, the wind will cause a flower to drop, and the bird will chirp in accord with the seasons.

Great King Asoka, who was deeply devoted to Buddhism and who did not, until just before his death at a great age, lose his power, offered a half a mango to an assembly of monks. It was only a small mango, but it gave the assembly great merit.

People who wish to be generous should clarify this principle and make an effort not to lose any opportunity to give generously. You indeed in your original nature possess the merit to give generously, and although each person may be different, each has the opportunity to practice generosity.

The Buddha said you should take generosity as your own; moreover, you should give it to your parents, your wives, and children. Even if you use it as your own, it will still be generosity and what your parents, wives, husbands, and children will gain will also be generosity. Even if you only possess a mere trace of generosity, you will have joy in your hearts, for it becomes that which you correctly transmit to others and this is done as a merit and a facet of the Buddha. Moreover, it is worthwhile even to practice one of the actions of a Bodhisattva.

You cannot change the minds of others, but if you give material gifts, you have a chance to show your mind of the Buddha Way and so can help it to change and experience the Way of enlightenment. To do this, you should certainly take a first step by beginning to practice generosity. In this way, generosity comes first among the six *paramitas* of the Bodhisattva. You cannot measure the size, great or small, of the mind, nor indeed can you measure the size of materials. There is, however, a time when mind changes materials and materials change mind. This is when both of them have generosity.

Loving and Compassionate Speech

Loving speech means that whenever you see sentient

beings, your compassion is aroused naturally and you use loving words. You cannot imagine using coarse speech. It is natural to ask about another's welfare when you greet him. In Buddhism you use the word *chincho* (to take care of yourself) and for older people there is the greeting *fushin* (how are you?). When you meet together and talk, you should care for each other, as you would do for a baby. With such a mind, you can speak truly—that is to say, you can speak compassionately. If someone has virtue you should praise it, and if they do not you should feel pity. If you love compassionate words, the action of loving words will increase. The compassionate words that are concealed in your daily life will emerge. Throughout life, in the present time, you should seek to speak compassionately. This doesn't mean seeking loving words from others, but giving them from your own hearts. You should never forget compassionate words either in this world or the next: they are the basis of the next life. To become friends with the enemy and to reconcile enemy kings should be the root of compassionate words. When you listen to loving words, you should face others, and that will make them happy and make them smile with joy. If you listen to loving words fully, you will impress your heart and spirit. You should realize that loving words come from the mind of love and that this mind is based on compassion. You should learn that loving words have great power to change situations and that they have greater virtue and meaning than mere praise.

Beneficial Action

Beneficial action means that you take care of every kind of person, no matter whether of high or low position, for this gives your life merit. You should think about people's present and future and about taking care of them so that they will develop merit.

A long time ago, during the Shin era in China, there was a man named Koyu who, on seeing a fisherman catch a turtle bought it and released it in the river. In the Gokan period, there was a man called Yoho who, as a boy, saved a sparrow at the foot of Mount Kain. When these people saw the turtle and the sparrow they simply felt sorry; they did not expect any special merit. They could not stop themselves from helping; their beneficial intent simply caused them to do so.

Foolish people think that if the other person's merit comes first, their own will lose out, but this is not true. Beneficial action is the one principle wherein you find no opposition between subjectivity and objectivity. It is a deed which gives merit to both.

There is a story from ancient times about King Shu. If a guest came when he was taking a bath or eating a meal, he would straighten his hair and receive the guest. He tried his best to give his merit to others without discriminating between people of different countries. He treated everyone in the same way. He took care of all people alike, no matter whether they bore him a grudge or were friendly.

If you do not have any discrimination, you can produce merit both for yourself and others. If you have such a mind, you can find it in natural phenomena such as grass, trees, wind and water. This mind should be resolved and always produce merit. Naturally, such beneficial intent considers foolish people and wishes to save them.

Identification with Others

Identification with others means not to differentiate self from others, in the manner of Shakyamuni, who was born and spent his whole life as a human being. He spent his entire life identifying with others, even in other worlds such as hells or the animal realms. When you identify with others, you are at one with yourself and others. There is an expression to be friends with the *koto* [Japanese musical instrument], poetry and sake. This means that as a human being you make friends with such things as music, poetry, and sake, and that they make friends with you. At times, you harmonize first with yourself, and, at times, first with others. The relationship between yourself and others is as endless as is your relationship with time.

Kanshi said: "The seas accept water without limit, thus creating great oceans, and mountains accept earth without limit, thus forming great mountain ranges."

In such a way, an outstanding king accepts all kinds of people, and thus he will have many people and countries in his rule. Such an outstanding king will become an emperor. An emperor does not dislike people, but this does not mean he will not give punishment or indeed prizes. Even when he punishes, he never dislikes the person he is punishing. Long ago, when people were simple and honest, there was no need for any punishment; things were different from the present. Even in the present day, some people seek the Way without expectation of reward or punishment, though foolish people cannot even imagine such an idea.

An outstanding king has a clear understanding of people's minds, and he does not reject nor discriminate against anyone. In this way, people gather round him, thus forming a country or state. They show the kind of mind which seeks an outstanding king. Average people, however, do not know the idea or principle of the nature of an outstanding king; they are simply happy if the king does not dislike or reject them.

Sometimes, not even being aware that the king will not reject them, they support him. In other words, a brilliant king and foolish people are able to live in harmony. In this manner, people ask the Bodhisattva for his support.

In all respects and wishes, the Bodhisattva practices in order to save sentient beings. What is most necessary is that you face everything with an open and flexible mind. All these four virtues—generosity, loving and compassionate words, beneficial action, and identification with others—possess and include each other. In this way, these virtues total sixteen.

Glossary

The following abbreviations are used: Chin. for Chinese; Jap. for Japanese; and Skt. for Sanskrit.

ANGO (Jap.) Literally, "dwelling in peace"; a period of intensive spiritual training in a Zen monastery or training center, usually ninety days in length.

ANUTTARA SAMYAK SAMBODHI (Skt.) Supreme unsurpassed awakening or wisdom.

ARHAT (Skt.) *Arhat* or *arahant* was originally a title given to people of high spiritual achievement. It was applied by the early Buddhists to one who had eliminated all defilements and had "no more to learn." *Arhat* practice was later contrasted to with the Bodhisattva's way, in which emphasis is on compassion for others.

AVALOKITESVARA *See* KANZEON

AVATAMSAKA SUTRA (Skt.; Chin. *Hua-yen Ching* ; Jap. *Kegon kyo*) Literally, garland sutra; the *Avatamsaka Sutra* is said to be the teachings of Shakyamuni Buddha during the three weeks immediately following his great enlightenment. It expounds the mutual interdependence and interpenetration of all phenomena and is the basic text of the *Hua-yen* school.

BODHI-MIND The mind in which an aspiration to enlightenment has been awakened.

BODHIDHARMA (Skt.; Jap. Daruma; d. 532) The twenty-eighth Dharma descendent of Shakyamuni Buddha, Bodhidharma was the Indian master who brought Zen to China, where he became known as the First Patriarch. According to tradition he sat facing a wall for nine years before transmitting the Dharma to Hui-k'o (Jap. Eka), the Second Patriarch in China (*Mumonkan*, Case 41).

261

BODHISATTVA (Skt.) Literally, "enlightened being"; one who practices the Buddha Way and compassionately foregoes final enlightenment for the sake of helping others become enlightened; the exemplar in Mahayana Buddhism.

BOKUSHU (Jap.; Chin. Mu-chou Ch'en-tsun-su, ca. 780–877) A great Chinese Zen master, Dharma successor to Obaku. It was Bokushu who first recognized Rinzai's potential and recommended to Obaku that he accept the young Rinzai as his student. Bokushu is also well known as Ummon's teacher.

BUDDHA (Skt.) Literally, "awakened one"; a term that variously indicates the historical Buddha, Shakyamuni; enlightened persons who have attained Buddhahood; and the essential truth, the true nature of all beings. *See* BUDDHA-NATURE and SHAKYAMUNI.

BUDDHA-DHARMA (Skt.; Jap. *buppo*) The true realization of life; the Way to follow in order to attain that realization according to the teachings of Shakyamuni Buddha.

BUDDHA-MIND *See* BODHI-MIND.

BUDDHA-NATURE The intrinsic nature of all beings; true nature, true self.

BUDDHAYANA (Skt.) *See* THREE YANAS.

DAIKAN ENO *See* SIXTH PATRIARCH.

DAI KENSHO (Jap.) This term refers to great enlightenment or the "Great Death" experience, seeing completely into one's true nature beyond all doubt. *See* KENSHO.

DAISAN (Jap.) *See* DOKUSAN.

DAI SHIN (Jap.) Great heart or mind, sometimes called Big Mind, where one is not functioning out of ego-centeredness.

DANA PARAMITA (Skt.) *See* PARAMITAS.

DENKOROKU (Jap.) Literally, "Record of the Transmission of the Light"; a collection of episodes from transmission situations in the history of the the lineage of fifty-two Patriarchs of the Soto school, from Mahakasyapa to Dogen Zenji, as recorded by Keizan Zenji. In some traditions the Denkoroku is employed in koan study. Cf. KEITOKU DENTO-ROKU.

DHARMA (Skt.) The teachings of Shakyamuni Buddha; Truth; Buddhist doctrine; universal law.

DHARMAKAYA (Skt.; Jap. *hosshin*) First of three aspects of Buddha-nature, known as the three bodies. *Dharmakaya* indicates the absolute beyond all discrimination; the inexpressible truth and transcendental reality; the unity of Buddha with all beings. The second aspect, *sambhogakaya,* refers to the Buddhas who manifest the powers arising from perfect enlightenment. The third, *nirmanakaya,* is Buddha-nature in human form acting for the benefit of sentient beings.

DHARMAS (Skt.) Phenomena; elements or constituents of existence.

DHARMA TALK *See* TEISHO.

DIAMOND SUTRA (Skt. *Vajracchedika Sutra* ; Jap. *Kongo kyo)* A text highly regarded by the Zen sect, it sets forth the doctrines of *shunyata* and *prajna.* The Sixth Patriarch attained enlightenment upon hearing a phrase from this sutra.

DOGEN KIGEN ZENJI (1200–1253) One of the greatest masters in the history of Zen, he brought the Buddha-dharma from China to Japan and is considered the founder of the Japanese Soto school. After training for nine years under Rinzai teacher Myozen, Dogen Zenji made the difficult journey to China, where he studied with and became Dharma successor to T'ien-t'ung Ju-ching (Jap. Tendo Nyojo) in the Soto Zen lineage. Dogen Zenji established Eihei-ji, the principal Soto training monastery, and is best known for his collection of Dharma essays, *Shobogenzo.*

DOKUSAN (Jap.) A one-to-one-encounter between Zen student and teacher in which the student's understanding is probed and stimulated and in which the student may consult the teacher on any matters arising directly out of practice.

EIGHT AWARENESSES The last teaching of Shakyamuni Buddha before his death. They are presented by Dogen Zenji as follows in *Hachi Dainin Gaku,* "The Eight Aspects of Enlightenment": (1) being free from greed, having few desires; (2) being satisfied with what one has; (3) enjoying quiet; (4) being diligent; (5) preserving correct remembrance; (6) practicing *samadhi*; (7) practicing Wisdom; (8) refraining from idle talk.

EKA (Chin. Hui-k'o) The Second Chinese Patriarch, who received the Dharma transmission from Bodhidharma. Eka is famous for his unstoppable determination to be Bodhidharma's student. When he implored Bodhidharma to pacify his mind, Bodhidharma asked Eka to show him this mind. When Eka returned after ten days of unceasing effort and asserted that he definitely could not find his mind, Bodhidharma confirmed that his mind had now been pacified.

EMPTINESS (Skt. *shunyata*) The fundamental nature of all phenomena.

GANTO (828–887) One of Tokusan's successors and a close Dharma brother of Seppo. Ganto's great shout as he died became an important koan for many who followed, including the great master Hakuin Zenji.

GENJOKOAN (Jap.) Literally, "Enlightenment Appears in Everyday Life"; one of the most well-known fascicles of *Shobogenzo* by Dogen Zenji.

GREAT DEATH *See* DAI KENSHO.

HAKUIN EKAKU ZENJI (1686–1769) The Patriarch of Japanese Rinzai Zen, through whom all present-day Rinzai masters have their lineage. He systematized koan study as we know it today and is known for his drawings and paintings, especially of Bodhidharma.

HEKIGANROKU (Jap.) Literally, "Blue Cliff Record"; Composed
about one hundred years earlier than the *Mumonkan,* this
koan collection is based on one hundred koans compiled
by Master Setcho (980–1052), who wrote a verse pointing
to the meaning of each koan. A century later, Master Engo
(1063–1135) added commentaries on each case and a
short poetic introduction to most of them. The name "Blue
Cliff Record" derives from a piece of calligraphy that hung
in Engo's room.

HINAYANA (Skt.) *See* THREE YANAS.

HUANG PO (Chin.) *See* OBAKU.

HUI-NENG *See* SIXTH PATRIARCH.

IDENTITY OF RELATIVE AND ABSOLUTE (Jap. *Sandokai*) One of the
most important Zen poems, this profound sutra is chanted
daily in Soto Zen services.

JIJUYU SAMADHI (Jap.-Skt. or JIJUYU-ZANMAI [Jap.]) Joyous, self-fulfilling *samadhi,* the touchstone of true Zen practice, which
has been transmitted from Buddha to Buddha down to the
present day. Cf. ZAZEN, SAMADHI.

JOSHU JUSHIN (Chin. Chao-chou Ts'ung-shen, 778–897) One of
the most important Chinese Zen masters, a Dharma successor of Nansen. Joshu was famous for his unique capacity to awaken students with brief verbal responses, called
"Joshu's lip and mouth Zen." Joshu appears in a number of
case koans and is most well known for his *mu. See also*
KOAN.

KALPA (Skt.) A term for an endlessly long period of time: if an
angel flew down once every hundred years and brushed its
wing across a solid rock one cubic mile in size, the rock
would be worn away before one kalpa had passed.

KANZEON (Jap., also Kannon or Kan Ji Sai Bosa; Skt. Avalokitesvara; Chin. Kuan-yin) Literally, "the one who hears the
sounds and cries, or supplications, of the world"; Kanzeon,
represented in the female form, is one of the principal

Bodhisattvas in Zen. Kanzeon manifests in whatever form is needed in order to respond to the needs of all beings.

KARMA (Skt.) The principle of causality, which holds that for every effect there is a cause and, in the human sphere, maintains that by our actions we determine the quality of our lives and influence the lives of others.

KATSU (Jap.) A Zen shout, originally used by the teacher when he wanted to sweep delusive thinking from the student's mind.

KEGON SUTRA (Jap.-Skt.) *See* AVALATAMSAKA SUTRA.

KEITOKU DENTO-ROKU (Jap.; Chin. Ching-te ch'uan-teng-lu) Literally, "Record Concerning the Passing on of the Lamp, composed in the Ching-te Period"; the earliest historical document in Zen literature, a thirty-volume work recounting deeds and sayings of over six hundred masters, composed by Tao-hsuan (Jap. Dosen) in the year 1004 A. D. Cf. DENKOROKU.

KEIZAN JOKIN ZENJI (1268–1325) The Fourth Patriarch of Japanese Soto Zen and the most important after Dogen Zenji. He became a monk under Dogen Zenji's disciple Koun Ejo and, after receiving the Dharma transmission, founded a number of monasteries throughout Japan including Soji-ji, one of the two primary Soto Zen monasteries in Japan today.

KENSHO (Jap.) Literally, "seeing into one's nature"; an experience of enlightenment, also known as *satori*.

KESA (Jap.; Skt. *Kasaya*) A monk's robe traditionally made out of abandoned rags cut into strips and stitched together, thus the expression "patch-robed monks" to refer to Zen monks.

KINHIN (Jap.) Walking zazen, usually done for five or ten minutes between periods of sitting zazen.

KOAN (Jap.; Chin. KUNG-AN) Literally, "public document"; in the Zen tradition, a statement, question, anecdote, or dialogue that cannot be understood or resolved intellectually.

Meditation on a koan leads one to transcend the intellect and experience the nondual nature of reality. Koans are given by the Zen teacher to bring students to realization and to help them clarify their understanding. Approximately seventeen hundred koans have been recorded from Chinese and Japanese sources. Many of these recount an exchange between master and student or a master's enlightenment experience and are known as "case koans." They can be found in various collections, most notably *The Gateless Gate* (*Mumonkan*), *The Blue Cliff Record* (*Hekiganroku*), *The Book of Equanimity* (*Shoyoroku*), and *The Book of the Transmission of the Lamp* (*Denkoroku*). *See also* DENKOROKU, HEKIGANROKU, KOAN STUDY, and MUMONKAN.

LOTUS SUTRA One of the most important Mahayana Buddhist texts, containing the doctrines of the transcendental nature of the Buddha and of the possibility for universal liberation.

MAHAKASYAPA (Skt.) became the Dharma successor of Shakyamuni Buddha when he alone smiled as Buddha silently held up a flower. Mahakasyapa was also renowned for ascetic self-discipline and took over leadership of the Sangha after Buddha's death.

MAHAYANA (Skt.) *See* THREE YANAS.

MANJUSRI (Skt.; Jap. Monju) The Bodhisattva of wisdom, often depicted riding a lion and holding a sword of wisdom that cuts through delusion. Especially appreciated in the Zen school, Manjusri Bodhisattva is the principal figure on the zendo altar.

MU (Jap., or *muji*) The character *mu* is a negative particle used in Zen to point directly at reality and has no discursive content. The use of the word in this sense originated with Joshu Jushin, who, when asked by a monk, "Does a dog have Buddha-nature?" directly answered, "*Mu!*" This incident is used as the opening koan in *The Gateless Gate* and is often the first koan encountered by Zen students in their koan study. The term *mu* is often used as a synonym for *emptiness*. *See also* KOAN.

MUMON EKAI (1183–1260) A student of Master Getsurin Shikan. After six years of working on Joshu's *Mu*, Mumon experienced *dai kensho* upon hearing the sound of a drum. He produced the koan collection best known in the West, *The Gateless Gate (Mumonkan)*, in which the first koan is Joshu's *Mu*. *See also* DAI KENSHO, KOAN, MU, MUMONKAN.

MUMONKAN (Jap.) *The Gateless Gate,* a major collection of koans consisting of forty-eight cases. *See also* KOAN, MUMON EKAI.

NANSEN FUGAN (Chin. Nan-ch'uan P'u-yuan, 748–835) one of the great Chinese Zen masters of the T'ang period, a Dharma successor of Baso and teacher of Joshu, who was the most renowned among his seventeen Dharma heirs. Nansen appears in a number of famous case koans in *Mumonkan* and *Hekiganroku*

NEMBUTSU (Jap.) Recitation of the name of Buddha with the intention of bringing about rebirth in the Pure Land.

NIRVANA (Skt.; Jap. *nehan*) A nondualistic state beyond life and death. The original meaning of the term was "to extinguish or burn out for lack of fuel," implying the complete exhaustion of all ignorance and craving. Extinction or burning out here conveys the sense of space being completely clear, no longer full of clouds and smoke. Nirvana sometimes refers specifically to the state of profound enlightenment attained by Buddha.

OBAKU (Jap.; Chin. Huang Po, d. 850) One of the greatest Chinese Zen masters, teacher of Rinzai and Bokushu.

PARAMITAS (Skt.) Literally, "gone to the other shore"; this term refers to the Six Perfections practiced by a Bodhisattva, culminating with *prajna paramita* ("perfection of wisdom"), which informs and fulfills the other five. The *paramitas* are a natural expression of the enlightened mind, the mind of meditation. The six *paramitas* are giving (*dana*), precepts or morality (*sila*), patience (*kshanti*), effort or vigor (*virya*), meditation (*dyhana*), and wisdom (*prajna*). Four more are sometimes added: skillfulness in means (*upaya*), determination (*pranidhana*), strength (*bala*), and knowledge (*jnana*).

PARINIRVANA (Skt.) Total extinction. Parinirvana is often equated with nirvana after death, but may simply refer to the death of a monk or nun.

PATRIARCH A term applied to all the Dharma successors who have received and formally transmitted the Buddha-dharma from Shakyamuni Buddha through twenty-eight generations in India and six generations in China down to Daikan Eno, the Sixth Chinese Patriarch. Since the Sixth Patriarch, the Dharma transmission has not been limited to just one successor, and anyone who has received the formal transmission of the Buddha-dharma down to the present day is a Patriarch.

PRAJNA (Skt.; Jap., *hannya*) Enlightened wisdom; wisdom that transcends duality of subject and object.

PRATYEKABUDDHA (Skt.) Literally, "solitary awakened one"; one who has attained enlightenment on his own and only for himself.

PRECEPTS (Skt. *sila*; Jap. *kai*) Buddhist teachings regarding personal conduct, which can be appreciated on a literal level as ethical guidelines and more broadly as aspects or qualities of reality itself. In Zen Buddhism, the precepts are as follows. The Three Treasures: be one with the Buddha; be one with the Dharma; be one with the Sangha. The Three Pure Precepts: do not commit evil; do good; liberate all sentient beings. The Ten Grave Precepts: refrain from killing; refrain from stealing; do not be greedy; refrain from telling lies; refrain from intoxication and ignorance; refrain from talking about others' errors and faults; do not elevate yourself by criticizing others; do not be stingy, especially with the Dharma; do not indulge in anger and hatred; do not speak ill of the Buddha, Dharma, or Sangha.

RINZAI GIGEN (Chin. Lin-chi I-hsuan, d. 866) Rinzai was one of the great masters of the Tang dynasty in China and the founder of the Rinzai school of Zen, noted for its emphasis on enlightenment and for its vigorous use of koans in zazen practice. Rinzai was a Dharma successor of Obaku.

ROSHI (Jap.) Literally, "old teacher"; an older Zen master; in the Soto tradition, a seasoned master at least fifty-two years old.

SAIJOJO ZEN (Jap.) Literally, "Supreme and Ultimate Vehicle Zen"; the most profound *dharmakaya* practice, the basis of Dogen Zenji's teaching. See also TANTRA and THREE YANAS.

SAMADHI (Skt.; Jap. *zanmai*) A state of mind characterized by one-pointedness of attention; a nondualistic state of awareness.

SAMSARA (Skt.) Literally, "stream of becoming"; the experience of suffering arising from ignorance. *Samsara* is reflected in the condition of our usual daily life, in which the main focus is perpetuation of the notion of a separate self.

SANGHA (Skt.) Originally referring to the community of Buddhist monks and nuns, the term *Sangha* later came to include laypersons who have received the precepts. In Zen, the term also connotes the harmonious interrelationship of all beings, phenomena, and events; in other words, the inseparability and harmonious working of Buddha-dharma.

SATORI (Jap.) *See* KENSHO.

SENSEI (Jap.) Title meaning "teacher."

SEPPO GISON (Jap.; Chin. Hsueh-feng I-ts'un, 822-908) Well-known Chinese Zen master, a successor of Tokusan. Seppo appears with his Dharma brother Ganto in a number of colorful koans and stories. He was famous as a *tenzo* (temple cook) and traveled from monastery to monastery with a big wooden spoon.

SESSHIN (Jap.) Literally, "to collect or settle the mind"; an intensive silent Zen meditation retreat.

SHAKYAMUNI (Skt.) Literally, "the sage of the Shakya clan"; this title is used to refer to Siddhartha Gautama, the historical Buddha, after his enlightenment.

SHASTRAS (Skt.) Philosophical commentaries composed by Mahayana thinkers that systematically interpret statements in the Buddhist sutras.

SHIKANTAZA (Jap.) Literally, "just sitting"; refers to zazen itself, without supportive devices such as breath-counting or koan study. Characterized by intense nondiscursive awareness, *shikantaza* is "zazen doing zazen for the sake of zazen."

SHOBO (Jap.) A term meaning "the true Dharma."

SHOBOGENZO (Jap.) Originally referred to the "True Dharma Eye" which Shakyamuni Buddha transmitted to Mahakasyapa; also the title of Dogen Zenji's great masterwork, "Treasury of the True Dharma Eye." It comprises some ninety-five fascicles dealing with a wide variety of Buddhist topics and is generally considered to be one of the most subtle and profound works in Buddhist literature.

SHUNYATA (Skt.) *See* EMPTINESS.

SIDDHI (Skt.) Supernatural ability that may appear as a by-product of spiritual development.

SKANDHAS (Skt.) Literally, "heaps" or "aggregates"; in Buddhist psychology, the five modes of being which, taken collectively, give rise to the illusion of self. They are: form, sensation, perception, discrimination, and awareness.

SIXTH PATRIARCH (Chin., Hui-neng; Jap. Eno, 638–713) Traditionally said to have been illiterate, Hui-neng was enlightened while still a layman upon overhearing a recitation of the Diamond Sutra. He became a Dharma successor of the Fifth Patriarch, Hung-gen, and all lines of Zen now existing descend from him. His teaching, as recorded in the *Platform Sutra,* stresses "sudden enlightenment" (as opposed to the "gradual enlightenment" of the Northern School of Ch'an, or Zen) and the identity of meditation (*dhyana*) and wisdom (*prajna*). He was largely responsible for the widespread flourishing of Zen in the T'ang dynasty.

SOTO SCHOOL The Zen lineage founded by Zen masters Tung-shan Liang-chieh (Jap. Tozan Ryokai, 807–869) and Ts'ao-shan Pen-chi (Jap. Sozen Honjaku, 840–901). The Japanese branch was founded by Zen masters Dogen Kigen (1200–1253) and Keizan Jokin (1268–1325).

SRAVAKA (Skt.) One who listens to the teachings, but leaves the teacher prematurely.

SUTRA (Skt.) Literally, "a thread on which jewels are strung"; Buddhist scripture; a dialogue or sermon attributed to Shakyamuni Buddha.

TANTRA (Skt.) Literally, "thread" or "continuity"; the study of Being: the intimate personal experience of reality. Tantra is the continuity that connects and transcends Hinayana, Mahayana, and Buddhayana (*See* THREE YANAS) and goes beyond all conventional concepts of sanity and compassion. In Japanese, this is called *Saijojo Zen,* the supreme and ultimate vehicle, the very basis of Dogen Zenji's teaching.

TAO (Chin.; Jap. *do*) Literally, the "Way," or "Path"; Tao is used to indicate Buddha-nature or the Way of or to enlightenment. Since Zen is a marriage between Indian Buddhism and Chinese Taoism, the term is historically significant.

TATHAGATA (Skt.) Literally, "thus coming, thus going," indicating the enlightened state, or "suchness"; one who has attained supreme enlightenment on the Way of Truth; one of the ten titles of the Buddha. Master Bankei said: "To neither come nor go, but to remain as you innately are, without allowing the mind to become obscured—this is what's meant by *Tathagata.*"

TEISHO (Jap.) A formal commentary by a Zen master on a koan or other Zen text. A *teisho* is nondualistic, which distinguishes it from an ordinary discursive lecture on some Buddhist topic.

Glossary

TENDO NYOJO (Jap.; Chin. T'ien-t'ung Ju-ching, 1163–1228) The
Chinese Soto Zen master under whom Dogen Zenji
attained awakening and from whom he received the true
Dharma transmission that he brought back to Japan.

THREE YANAS (Skt.) Literally, "three vehicles," by which a practitioner can travel on the way to enlightenment. Hinayana,
the Lesser Vehicle, corresponds to a strict and narrow
interpretation of Buddha's teachings, with a goal of enlightenment for oneself alone. Mahayana, the Greater Vehicle, is
not confined to a literal interpretation of Buddha's teachings. The Mahayana interpretation is broad and flexible,
recognizing no fixed or absolute codes of belief and conduct, but rather responding to each situation according to
the unique circumstances. It is the way of the Bodhisattva,
who vows to liberate all sentient beings. Buddhayana, the
Dharmakaya Vehicle, arises from One-Buddha-mind
Wisdom: absolute nonduality and nonseparation of self
and other. It is the most supremely accomplished and vast
of the Three Yanas.

TOKUSAN (Jap.; Chin. Te-shan Hsuan-chien, 781?–867) A most
influential teacher, from whom nine major Zen masters
received Dharma transmission. After living for a long time
in seclusion, Tokusan became famous for the compassionate severity of his training: "Thirty blows if you speak, thirty blows if you do not!"

UPAYA (Skt.) Skillful or expedient means, usually referring to the
ways that masters work with their students to bring them
to awakening.

VAIROCHANA BUDDHA (Skt.) Literally, "He Who Is Like the Sun";
one of the five transcendent Buddhas.

WU, EMPEROR When Bodhidharma first arrived in China, he was
invited to the Buddhist Emperor Wu's court. Much to the
emperor's regret ever afterward, he did not realize who
Bodhidharma was and could not grasp the significance of
his teaching (*Hekiganroku*, Case 1). Later on, after

273

Bodhidharma had departed, Emperor Wu's daughter was sent by her father to study with him, and she became one of his four major disciples.

ZAZEN (Jap.) Literally, *za* means "sitting" and *zen* (Chin. ch'an) stands for "meditation" or "*samadhi*"; the practice of Zen meditation. *Zazen* was originally a tentative term to indicate *jijuyu samadhi*, referred to as "zazen" because people who saw Bodhidharma sitting facing a wall at Shorin Temple on Mt. Suzan did not understand that he was practicing *jijuyu samadhi*. The posture of his practice was similar to that of *dhyana* (meditation or contemplation) described by the Buddhist scholars of the time. Therefore his practice was commonly called "zazen" and his successors were called followers of the Zen school.

ZEN (Jap., abbreviation for *zenna*; Chin. *ch'an* or *ch'anna*; Skt. *dhyana*) An abbreviation for *zazen*, indicating the school of those who practice *zazen*. This school developed from the fusion of Indian Buddhism and Chinese Taoism when Bodhidharma brought the true Dharma to China, probably in the first half of the sixth century. *See also* BODHIDHARMA, JIJUYU SAMADHI, ZAZEN. Zen is characterized in a famous four-line verse attributed to Bodhidharma:

> A special transmission outside the scriptures
> No dependence on words or letters.
> Seeing directly into the mind of man
> Realizing true nature, becoming Buddha.

ZENDO (Jap.) A meditation hall for the practice of zazen.

ZENJI (Jap.) Literally, "Zen master"; a title applied to the head of each Zen school; a term of great respect given to the most renowned and accomplished masters.

References

Dogen Zenji. *Shobogenzo,* translated by Kosen Nishiyama, Tokyo: Nakayama Shobo, 1983.

Fischer-Schreiber, Ehrhard, Friedrichs, and Diener. *Encyclopedia of Eastern Philosophy and Religion.* Boston: Shambhala, 1989.

Fischer-Schreiber, Ehrhard, and Diener. *The Shambhala Dictionary of Buddhism and Zen,* translated by Michael H. Kohn. Boston: Shambhala, 1991.

Huang Po. *The Zen Teaching of Huang Po,* edited and translated by John Blofeld. London: The Buddhist Society, 1971.

Kodera, Takashi James. *Dogen's Formative Years in China.* Boulder: Prajna Press, 1980.

Kongtrul, Jamgon. *The Torch of Certainty.* Boston: Shambhala, 1977.

Maezumi, Hakuyu Taizan and John Daido Loori. *The Way of Everyday Life.* Los Angeles: Center Publications, 1978.

Merzel, Dennis Genpo. *The Eye Never Sleeps: Striking to the Heart of Zen.* Boston: Shambhala, 1991.

Mitchell, Stephen. *The Gospel According to Jesus.* New York: Harper Collins, 1991.

Okamura, Shohaku. *Dogen Zen.* Kyoto, Japan: Kyoto Soto Zen Center, 1988.

Okamura, Shohaku. *Shikantaza: An Introduction to Zazen.* Kyoto, Japan: Kyoto Soto Zen Center, 1985.

Rinzai, *The Record of Rinzai,* translated by Irmgard Schloegl. London: The Buddhist Society, 1975.

Sekida, Katsuki, translator & editor. *Two Zen Classics: Mumonkan & Hekiganroku.* New York: Weatherhill, 1977.

Shibayama, Zenkei. *Zen Comments on the Mumonkan.* New York: Harper & Row, 1974.

Tanahashi, Kazuaki, ed. *Moon in a Dewdrop: Writings of Zen Master Dogen.* San Francisco: North Point Press, 1985.

Trungpa, Chogyam. *Cutting Through Spiritual Materialism.* Boston: Shambhala, 1987.

Yokoi, Yuho with Victoria, Daizen. *Zen Master Dogen.* New York: Weatherhill, 1976.

If you wish to receive further information on Zen training under the guidance of Dennis Genpo Merzel, in Europe or the United States, please contact:

Kanzeon Zen Center Utah
1274 E. South Temple
Salt Lake City, Utah 84102
Tel: (801) 328–8414